The Gymnastics Book

The Young Performer's Guide to Gymnastics

2ND EDITION

Elfi Schlegel & Claire Ross Dunn

FIREFLY BOOKS

A Firefly Book

Published by Firefly Books Ltd. 2012

First printing

Publisher Cataloging-in-Publication Data (U.S.)

Schlegel, Elfi.
The gymnastics book : the young performer's guide to gymnastics / Elfi Schlegel ; Claire
Ross Dunn.
2nd ed.
[144] p. : col. photos. ; cm.
Includes index.
ISBN-13: 978-1-77085-160-3
ISBN-13: 978-1-77085-133-7 (pbk.)
1. Gymnastics--Juvenile literature. I. Dunn, Claire Ross. II. Title.
796.44dc23   GV464.5.S354 2012

Library and Archives Canada Cataloguing in Publication

Schlegel, Elfi
The gymnastics book : the young performer's guide
to gymnastics / Elfi Schlegel, Claire Ross Dunn. -- 2nd ed.
Includes index.
ISBN 978-1-77085-160-3 (bound). -- ISBN 978-1-77085-133-7 (pbk.)
1. Gymnastics--Juvenile literature. I. Dunn, Claire Ross
II. Title.
GV464.5.S34 2012   j796.44   C2012-902183-0

Published in the United States by
Firefly Books (U.S.) Inc.
P.O. Box 1338, Ellicott Station
Buffalo, New York 14205

Published in Canada by
Firefly Books Ltd.
66 Leek Crescent
Richmond Hill, Ontario L4B 1H1

Cover and interior design: Hartley Millson

Printed in China

The publisher gratefully acknowledges the financial support for our publishing program
by the Government of Canada through the Canada Book Fund as administered by the
Department of Canadian Heritage.

Picture Credits

All photos by Jolie Dobson except those
appearing on:

p. 4, 15, 103, 130, courtesy of Elfi Schlegel

p. 8, 15, 103, 114, 115, 117, 118, 135, scrap
book paper design by AKaiser/Shutterstock

p. 8, University of Florida Athletic
Association

p. 98, courtesy of Debbie Boycott

p.104, REUTERS/Hans Deryk (China)

p. 114, Wally McNamee/CORBIS (top),
Bettman/CORBIS (bottom)

p. 112, 115, Neal Preston/CORBIS (top),
Marc Francott/TempSport/CORBIS (bottom)

p. 116, AP Photo/Kevork Djansezian

p. 118, courtesy of Tim Daggett

p. 119, Special Olympics Ontario

p. 120, 124, 125, Grace Chiu/GraceClik

p. 121, courtesy of Shawn Johnson

p. 122, Norm Loader

p. 123, Patrick Schneider/Charlotte
Observer/KRT/Abaca

p. 126, REUTERS/Carlos Barria (Brazil)

p. 128, Tom Warren

p. 133, Fédération Internationale de
Gymnastique (logo and graphic)

p. 135, CP PHOTO/COC/R. Warren

p. 138, Richard Termine Costumes:
Dominique Lemieux © 2007 Cirque du
Soleil Inc.

Contents

Preface

One Saturday in 1972, I wandered away from my arts and crafts class at the local recreation center and opened the doors to the gymnasium. Behind them I discovered what would become my playground for the next 15 years.

My first year was spent in a recreational gymnastics program—a one-hour weekly affair that my mother observed from the back of the gym. A few years later, at age 10, I began to take gymnastics more seriously. I was named to the Ontario provincial team and competed in the Canadian National Championships. I finished 10th—a result that surprised many, including me—and I was described as the most promising gymnast in Canada. From then on I wanted to become an Olympian.

Watching Nadia Comaneci at the 1976 Montreal Olympics taught me what it would take to make my dreams a reality. My teammates and I watched from the stands in awe while Nadia racked up all those perfect 10s. From that day on, if my coach asked me to practice a routine a dozen times, I did so willingly.

In 1978, I was crowned Canadian National Champion, won 2 gold medals at the Commonwealth Games and became a member of the World Championship Team. A year later, Canada celebrated a monumental victory, winning gold over the United States at the Pan American Games in Puerto Rico. I was one step closer to my Olympic dream. Then came disaster: the 1980 Olympic boycott. Although Canada decided to hold an Olympic Team tryout (and I qualified), I remember thinking that it was a futile exercise. Most of my friends at the elite level were tired and disappointed. Some had even left the sport. I too considered quitting.

My father encouraged me to focus on a college scholarship instead. At the University of Florida, I became a six-time All-American and placed third in the all-around at the 1985 NCAA Championships. Although I eventually left the sport on my own terms, I was able to savor my success.

Gymnastics has given me the opportunity to travel all over the world and make many new friends. It's also allowed me to turn gymnastics into a job, working as a commentator, first for CBC and CTV, and now for NBC Sports. But perhaps most importantly, it's given me the chance to open my own gymnastics club in Oakville, Ontario with my younger sister Andrea. For the last 15 years there I've taught what I've learned, and in turn, I have learned new things from the budding gymnasts who participate in our programs.

This is an updated version of *The Gymnastics Book*. We have updated the skills section with what's new in gymnastics, and we've added a wider range of skills, from basic exercises to some that are more challenging. If you're just trying out gymnastics for the first time, this book is for you. If you're working on your first one-handed cartwheel or round off, then this book is for you, too! We've also added tips, stories and memories from a few experienced competitive gymnasts, so you can read about what makes them tick and the secrets to their success.

I am delighted to take you on a fun, exciting journey into the world of gymnastics. Welcome!

Elfi Schlegel

Elfi Schlegel, age 12, representing Canada for the first time at the "Milk Meet" Competition, Toronto's Maple Leaf Gardens, 1976.

CHAPTER 1

Choosing Gymnastics

There are so many great reasons to choose gymnastics—and if you're reading this, you probably don't need much convincing. What's not to love about the world of gymnastics? There's flying, jumping, spinning, flipping… and so many different kinds of equipment to use.

People talk about playing basketball, playing football and playing soccer but no one ever says, "I play gymnastics." I think maybe they should. People are often turned off by the hard work they think it will be to learn the sport of gymnastics. They worry that they're too tall. They worry that they're not small enough, flexible or coordinated enough. But I say, none of this matters. You don't have to be an elite athlete to get involved.

I love "playing gymnastics." And there are lots of other benefits, too. No matter who you are, you can have fun and improve your health, flexibility, balance, agility, spatial orientation and coordination, all by leaps and bounds. You can learn the basics of gymnastics and then expand into some of its fun options, like rhythmic gymnastics or trampoline. Everyone can do it, from babies all the way up to the master's level. You can earn university scholarships with gymnastics, and even travel the world with the sport. You don't have to be an Olympian to do all that—but you will have fun!

Here are some of the great things gymnastics has to offer.

A Sport of All Sports

If you are involved in sports like diving and skating, your coach may encourage you to learn gymnastics to build your strength, flexibility, balance, coordination, agility and self-confidence.

But gymnastics will make you a better athlete no matter what sport you like. The great thing about gymnastics is that everyone can enjoy the activity—not just certain athletes building certain skills. Gymnastics doesn't just improve strength and flexibility—it also has positive effects on other aspects of your life. Gymnastics enhances all your skills. It also teaches you motivation: how to try, try again until you're happy with one skill and are able to move on to the next one.

Bianca Dancose-Giambattisto, an elite Canadian gymnast who shares all kinds of insider tips and stories in Chapter 9, says, "gymnastics is a global sport and extremely beneficial for my health in every manner. Balance, coordination, cardio, speed, power, strength, flexibility and grace are all trained. Gymnastics touches every part of the body, and keeps gymnasts very balanced muscle-wise." I absolutely agree.

A Sport for All Ages

People of all ages can benefit from gymnastics. Whether you are 2 years old attending Kindergym with a caregiver, or an adult learning gymnastics for the first time, gymnastics will help improve your flexibility and strength. It would be ideal to start learning gymnastics early in life, but it's never too late to start.

A Sport with No Gender Bias

One of the best things about gymnastics is that it's open to everyone. The apparatus—that is, the equipment used in the sport of artistic gymnastics—doesn't discriminate. From rings to balance beam, females and males are equally capable and welcome. At the Olympic level, however, only women compete on the balance beam and only men compete on the pommel horse, though anyone can enjoy these events at a recreational level. Balance, coordination and strength are qualities that should be pursued by everyone.

A Sport That's The Right Fit

If you've ever watched the very best gymnasts compete in the Olympics on TV, then you know what the pinnacle of the sport looks like. The Olympics is the dream for every athlete. But don't worry initially about having to leap over an Olympic-sized vault, or use a beam four feet off the ground. Recreational facilities typically offer scaled-down, recreational-sized equipment. You can always progress to competition-sized apparatuses later.

Elfi's scrapbook

Neal Anderson—a college football draft for the Chicago Bears in the 1980s—was a running back for the University of Florida at the same time I was there on a gymnastics scholarship. Neal loved to watch our competitions. Sometimes he would join our practices and use the spring floor to practice tumbling. Neal's interest in the "Sport of all Sports" theory was to practice gymnastics so he could perform back flips on the football field whenever he scored a touchdown—in full football gear!

8

The Gymnastics Family

The gymnastics family has several branches: artistic and rhythmic gymnastics, trampoline, and exciting new alternatives such as sport aerobics, sport acrobatics, tumbling and cheerleading. In artistic gymnastics, various skills are performed on an apparatus. Women perform on the vault, uneven bars, balance beam and floor. Men perform on the floor, pommel horse, still rings, vault, parallel bars and horizontal bar. In rhythmic gymnastics, skills are performed with an apparatus such as a rope, hoop, ball, ribbon and clubs. This book will focus on artistic gymnastics, given it is typically what you'll encounter at the beginner recreational level.

Above all, the sport of gymnastics is about fun, fitness and fundamentals:

FUN because it's fun to jump, tumble and swing;

FITNESS because you'll gain flexibility, strength, power, muscular and cardiovascular endurance, balance, agility, coordination, body awareness and spatial orientation; and, above all,

FUNDAMENTALS because the moves you will learn—landings, stationary positions, locomotions, swings, rotations and springs—can be applied to almost any sport.

Knowing What to Look For

So. You've decided to start gymnastics. Now what?
Where do you go? What do you look for?

Your first step will be to discuss your goals with your parent or caregiver. Once you've identified what your goals are, looking for the right club and coach will be much easier.

Identifying Your Goals

What do you hope to learn, and how much time do you want to spend learning it? Do you want to be a recreational gymnast as well as explore other activities? Do you want to use gymnastics to become more flexible for skating or other sports? Do you want to be the next Nadia Comaneci, and redefine the sport of gymnastics?

If you're not sure of the answers just yet, don't worry; it may be too early to tell. The most important thing to know is whether you want to pursue a recreational or competitive program. Once you've figured that out, it will be easier to take the next step: choosing a club.

Choosing a Club

You have two options in terms of gymnastics facilities: public or private.

Public Facilities

Throughout most of North America, the YMCA and Parks and Recreation offer basic, recreational gymnastic programs. In the United States, Boys' and Girls' Clubs of America also offer various courses. Although the cost of public facilities is generally less than that of private clubs, staff members in public facilities usually do not have comparable qualifications to the staff who work in private facilities.

Private Facilities

Private gymnastics clubs focus solely on gymnastics. As a result, they typically offer a wider range of programs and specialize in coaching at both recreational and competitive levels.

If any of your friends already takes gymnastics, ask for recommendations about local clubs. You can also contact the Gymnastics Federation for local referrals, or check the Internet (see page 143 for sites). Then conduct your own research. The better informed you are, the better choice you'll make.

Signing Up

Once you've found a facility you like, you need some information before signing up. First, find out about the facility's philosophy and program goals. Do they match yours? Most clubs provide a brochure that outlines their programs; if they don't, discuss the following issues with a member of their staff:

✔ Is the facility committed to teaching kids your age?

✔ What are the facility's safety policies and procedures? Are there regular safety and maintenance checks of the equipment?

✔ What are the costs and duration of the program?

✔ Can you observe a class, and are there drop-ins? Are any participants/caregivers available to answer questions and share experiences?

✔ How long has the facility been in operation? Clearly, a club with an established reputation is ideal, but if it is new, ensure that the club has solid credentials.

✔ Is the building clean? After all, you want to feel comfortable running around in your bare feet.

✔ How large is the facility? Remember, bigger isn't always better. Smaller facilities cater directly to recreational athletes, and the equipment is specifically designed for recreational programs. Although some facilities offer competitive-specific equipment, you won't need it if you're only learning the fundamentals of the sport.

✔ What sort of insurance coverage does membership include, and what fees are necessary for full coverage? If any injury occurs, does the facility guarantee full treatment, both upon occurrence and through rehabilitation?

Choosing a Coach

It's also important to make inquiries about the coaching staff. After all, a great program starts with a great teacher.

✔ Does the coach have a gymnastics coaching certificate? In Canada, both recreational and competitive coaches must be certified by the National Coaching Certification Program (NCCP). Contact your local gymnastics federation for recommendations on clubs.

✔ Are the coaches trained in first aid and CPR?

✔ How many years of coaching experience do the coaches have? In particular, ask about their experience coaching children. A coach must have the required skills or be supervised by a more experienced coach before leading a class by him- or herself.

✔ Above all, you want coaches with great personality. The coach should be clear, positive, enthusiastic, and have a sense of humor. After all, you're there to have fun! They should also help you feel comfortable, while teaching you new things and encouraging you to progress at your own pace.

Choosing a Program

Ask about the programs that are offered. Here's what to look for:

✔ What are the program's expectations? Is a certain level of experience required? Are programs available for your experience level?

✔ Can you join a class with your own age group? Usually, classes have a two- or three-year age range. You'll have more fun with the right age group, and the program will be tailored to you.

✔ What is the frequency and length of the classes? Think about your interests and your level of commitment, and choose a program accordingly.

✔ Are lesson plans available? All good programs have them. A lesson plan should be gauged to the ability of the class and be progression-oriented. Each step must be mastered before the next one can be tackled.

✔ What is the student-coach ratio? For children 5 years of age and older, the ratio should not exceed 10 to 1, although ideally it should be 8 to 1. For Kindergym (ages 18 months to 4), the ratio should not exceed 8 to 1, ideally 6 to 1.

Registration

Find out when to register for the facility's programs. Usually, clubs will assign specific dates for registration. Don't miss the deadline—lots of fun awaits!

CHAPTER 3

Getting Started

So, you've selected your club, observed a class, enjoyed attending a drop-in class, you've finally registered and now your first day is fast approaching. What's next?

Expectations

The first gymnastics class can be very exciting, but it may also be overwhelming. Even if you're normally outgoing, you may feel shy on your first day. Here are some ways to ease your first-day jitters:

✔ Visit the facility in advance to get to know the program and staff (attend a drop-in).

✔ Arrive ahead of time.

✔ And remember, everyone starts as a beginner. Just have fun and be a good sport!

Safety

If you have long hair, tie it back so it doesn't get caught in the equipment. For the same reason, never wear jewelry or any other adornments during gymnastics.

Bare feet are advised rather than shoes, slippers or other footwear, as injuries can occur due to slipping and sliding in footwear.

What to Wear

Unless your gymnastics club requires you to buy a uniform, you can probably make do with your own clothes. Loose cotton shorts and a T-shirt are just fine, as are tights or yoga pants.

After you've been to a few classes, you may find that one outfit becomes your favorite and just feels right in the gym; consider purchasing duplicates. Always remember to set out your gym gear the night before class.

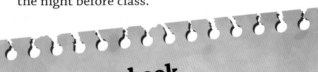

Elfi's scrapbook

I remember the anticipation of my first gymnastics class. I talked about it all week. I'm sure my parents were relieved when the day finally arrived. My mother sat at the back of the gym, watching the first hour of a sport that would eventually consume 15 years of my life. Little did we know!

CHAPTER 4

The Healthy Gymnast

"**Y**our body is your temple."

"You are what you eat."

We've all heard these sayings, and they're true. If you eat too much, your body won't perform. If you don't eat enough, your body won't have the fuel it needs. And if you eat junk food—well, the term says it all. Gymnastics is physically demanding, so it makes sense to eat properly and take care of your body.

Nutrition: Fueling the Machine

It is just as important for the once-a-week gymnast to practice good nutrition as it is for the competitive athlete pursuing the Olympic dream. Eating properly before a class will get you through lots of physical activity and assist in sustaining your energy level for the entire session.

Remember to drink lots of water before and after class to prevent dehydration. This is especially true during the summer when you're sweating excessively from the heat.

Thirty minutes before practice, eat a small snack instead of a full meal. Too much food will make you feel sluggish and tired. Fruit, vegetables, crackers and cheese, yogurt and juice are all good choices. Junk food is not. Junk food provides no nutritional value. Instead, you will experience a jittery "sugar high" that will leave you unfocused and without sustenance for your class. Eating properly helps you focus and maximize your fitness.

Eating well will help you feel good and will enhance your performance. And if you get into competitive gymnastics, you'll really need to fuel the machine with proper nutrition. To read about what elite athletes eat during training, see Chapter 10.

Gymnastics:
The Whole Body Workout

Gymnastics is considered "the whole body workout" because it exercises every part of your body, right and left sides. It also gives you strength and muscle awareness. This is about yanking your eyes from a screen, putting down the remote, shutting off your cell phone, and exercising more than your texting thumbs. In fact, Canadian National Team gymnast Bianca Dancose-Giambattisto's New Year's resolution was "less time on Facebook and cell phones... way too time consuming."

Dr. Larry Nassar is the United States Association of Gymnastics (USAG) National Medical Coordinator, the Women's Artistic National Team Doctor and the President of the Gymnastics Doctor Autism Foundation. Dr. Nassar spoke to me about the benefits of gymnastics for everyone, including children and special needs athletes:

> Recreational gymnastics enhances your strength and flexibility, but the benefits don't stop there. You learn how to control your strength and flexibility by enhancing your sense of balance and kinesthetic awareness. This means you learn coordination and have a better understanding of where your arms and legs are in relation to your trunk. Eye contact with coaches and peers is improved, along with spatial awareness. Your abilities to listen and follow directions are nurtured. You learn to take turns and play together with peers. This type of play improves cognition, which helps with problem solving and attention to task. Research has shown that children who participate in recreational gymnastics classes have increased bone mineral density compared to children who do not do gymnastics. Overall, recreational gymnastics enhances the physical and social abilities of children.
>
> What makes recreational gymnastics even more impressive is the growing involvement of children with physical, emotional and mental disabilities. These same characteristics of recreational gymnastics make it an ideal activity for children with special needs. Many gymnastics clubs throughout the world have opened their doors to children with special needs. With guidance, a gymnastics club may be thought of as a large therapy center that takes the child out of a more "sterile" medical environment and places them into a more "sporting" environment.
>
> Many children with special needs may be able to benefit from this more inclusive environment. Children with special needs have not only shown enhanced motor skills, but also improved social skills. Gymnastics coaches and gymnasts in these clubs that have special needs programs have reported that they too benefit from working with and alongside these special needs children. The reciprocal nourishment among all involved leaves everyone with a sense of enhanced wellbeing. Special needs children are looked at from a sense of potential instead of problem. When special needs children enter the world of recreational gymnastics, they are walking down a path of potential.

Whoever you are, wherever you live, whatever your level of experience, gymnastics will make your body feel great—and you'll feel great, too.

Warming Up

Warming Up

Cardiovascular activity helps move blood to the muscles to warm them up and prepare them for work. Cardiovascular exercise will help you to work up a light sweat and increase your heart rate.

Before and after each class, it's important to follow a regular warm-up and cool-down routine. You can periodically change your warm-up routine so you don't get bored. It's fun to regularly do these warm-ups, cool-downs and stretches at home, too.

Getting Started

Warming up is an activity that you can do in large or small groups. The emphasis in warming up should be on fun, participatory activities where no one gets eliminated. These activities should keep you in constant motion and keep you engaged.

The warm-up may take about 15 minutes to complete: 10 minutes of cardio (that means getting your heart pumping), and 5 minutes of stretching.

Examples of a cardio warm-up include skipping, hopping, jumping, speed changes, relays, changing levels and direction—anything that focuses on agility and gets your whole body moving.

STRETCHING

Now your body is prepared for stretching. This part of your routine lasts about 5 minutes. Hold each stretch for several seconds. Never bounce, and be careful to ease in and out of each move.

STRADDLE STRETCH

Sit comfortably on the floor with your legs apart. Keep your legs straight, knees facing the ceiling. Turn to one side and reach both arms along one leg, stretching toward your toes. Keep your chin up. Walk your arms in front of your body when switching sides. Repeat twice on each side, holding for 3 to 5 seconds each time.

PSOAS STRETCH

The psoas is a hip flexor muscle. To do this stretch, kneel on one knee and place your other leg in front, bending at the knee. Place your hands on either side of your leg. Lean forward, but keep your chest and head up. Make sure your knee doesn't go over your toes. Hold this position for at least 30 seconds. If you don't feel much stretch, slowly move your foot out and away from your body. Repeat with each leg.

HAMSTRING STRETCH

You can do this stretch while you're performing the psoas stretch. From the psoas stretch position, push your body back so that your hips are directly over your supporting knee. Stretch out your front leg, keeping your hands on either side of your body. Hold the stretch for 30 seconds. To make this stretch more challenging, flex your front foot toward the ceiling.

CHAPTER 6

Skills

"Skill" is the term used to define a single gymnastic movement that can be combined to create a routine of 2 or more elements. Every skill discussed in this chapter can be used as a basic gymnastic move that can then be adapted for more advanced moves. Just remember, photos and words can never do justice to the real thing. So it's important to practice at the gym.

In artistic gymnastics, skills are performed on an apparatus. Women perform on the vault, uneven bars, balance beam and floor. Men perform on the floor, pommel horse, still rings, vault, parallel bars and horizontal bar. This is the Olympic order of events.

Here, we'll start with the floor exercise elements, because many of them can transfer over to other apparatuses.

THE BASICS

BRAKES AND LANDING

Brake or Stop Position

To "put on the brakes" is to execute a landing in proper position. Absorb the landing with your knees, chest up, feet shoulder-width apart. This is the basic landing position on or off all apparatuses.

SAFETY FALL

1 *Stand up, arms crossed.*

2 *Roll back.*

3 *Stand up.*

It's okay to fall. Landing, or falling, is an integral part of gymnastics. Just as in skating or snowboarding, kids in gymnastics are taught how to fall properly and to easily get up and go again. When you practice your safety fall, cross your arms in front of your chest. Jump up, squat down to the ground, roll onto your back, and rock forward again to stand up.

THE BASICS

BASIC POSITIONS: TUCK

Tuck: hold your knees to your chest.

Tuck, pike and straddle are some of the most common positions used in gymnastics, and are carried over from apparatus to apparatus.

PIKE

Pike: stretch your legs out in front, and reach your hands to your toes.

STRADDLE

Straddle: open your legs, hands stretched apart and in front of your body.

START POSITION, FINISH POSITION

The start and finish positions are different for boys and girls. Girls stand with legs together, arms stretched high and palms facing out. Boys stand with legs together but with arms either stretched high, palms facing in, or with one arm high and the other arm by their side.

LUNGE

From a stand, step forward with one leg (whichever you prefer), foot slightly turned out, knee slightly bent, back leg straight, hips facing forward, arms stretched up in a finish position, with palms facing back.

THE BASICS

TIGHT BODY

Banana position (lying on your back).

Superman position (lying on your front).

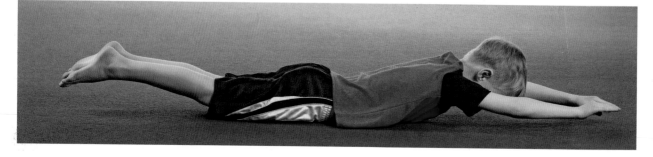

Everything in gymnastics is about a tight body. We tell our gymnasts, "no cooked spaghetti!" To develop core stability and strength, you need to be aware of your muscles from head to toe, and know how to keep them in control.

There is an important safety reason why you learn how to keep a tight body. Let's say you're about to do a move where you land onto your arms. If you were to let your arm muscles weaken, you might find yourself flat on your face! Tight body—a key position to know.

LOCOMOTION

1-foot hop

There are several ways to move your body. Some examples include running, hopping, jumping with two feet, skipping, cat leaps, scissor leaps and split leaps.

31

FLOOR EXERCISE

Recreational floor skills can be taught with the aid of an incline or wedge mat as well as blocks. Eventually, you can progress to the floor. Here are a few common floor skills along with their progressions. These are the basics you'll need to create combinations.

Rolls

LOG ROLL

To complete this move, maintain a straight and tight body position. (Remember? "No cooked spaghetti!") The log roll can be performed on an incline mat, level floor mat or wedge mat.

Begin by lying down on the wedge mat with your body straight and fully extended, and your arms over your head. Roll your entire body, like a pencil, down the mat. Continue rolling on the floor or wedge, maintaining a tight body position. Repeat this move, rolling up the wedge to increase the difficulty. You can also do a sideward variation by tucking your knees into your chest.

FORWARD ROLL

1 Stand on the high end of the wedge.

2 Tuck chin into chest and push off to roll over.

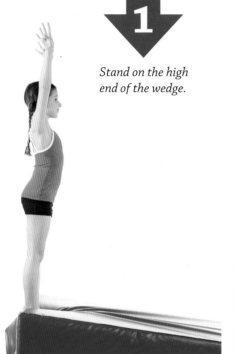

3 Finish in a straight stand.

Stand on the high end of the wedge. Squat down, bending at your knees and hips and place your hands flat, shoulder-width apart, in front of your feet. Raise your hips and tuck your chin into your chest. Push off your feet, roll over and finish in a straight stand.

FLOOR EXERCISE

STRADDLE FORWARD ROLL

Push off hands and stand in straddle to finish.

In a variation to the forward roll, stand with your feet in a straddle position. Extend your hands between your legs on the mat and perform a forward roll, tucking your chin to your chest. Finally, as shown in this photo, push off your hands and stand in a straddle to finish.

PIKE FORWARD ROLL

Getting up out of the pike forward roll.

Stand with your feet together, arms raised high. Reach your arms toward the ground while keeping your legs straight. Follow through the roll action by tucking your chin to chest and rolling onto your back, continuing to keep your legs straight. Place your arms on the outside of your legs to help push off your hands to a stand. Remember that your legs must maintain a stretched position throughout the roll.

BACKWARD ROLL

1

Squat position.

Squat on the high end of the wedge. Stretch your arms in front and roll backwards, keeping your knees and chin into your chest. Let your arms hit the mat first, palms down, to protect your head. Your arms will help push you all the way over, followed by the rest of your body. Finish in a stand.

2

Roll backwards.

3

Let arms help to push over, into a stand.

FLOOR EXERCISE

Handstand

The handstand is a key gymnastics skill. You'll see it time and time again on most apparatuses. Try to master these progressions before attempting a handstand.

FRONT SUPPORT

This position resembles the start of a push-up position. Your body should look like a table. Shoulders are in line with hands. Hands should be shoulder-width apart.

FRONT SUPPORT WITH FEET RAISED

Assume a front support position on the floor as if you were going to do push-ups. Now raise your feet on a block. Practice this a few times, keeping the core of your body tight and stretched.

WALK UP THE MAT

Mid-walk up the wall.

Place a mat against a wall. In a front support position, walk your feet up the wall as far as you are comfortable. Maintain a tight body position, avoiding an arch in the lower back. While your feet are moving, walk your hands closer toward the wall. Hold this position comfortably. Don't fall out of the handstand position. Maintain your strength as you walk down.

Partial handstand.

Finish in a handstand position.

FLOOR EXERCISE

HANDSTAND SWITCH KICK

Start in a stand position with one foot in front, arms raised above your head. Lower your body and hands toward the floor with your foot still in front. At the moment your hands touch the floor, raise your back foot off the floor. Put pressure onto your hands, kicking your back foot, switching with your support foot in the air. Push off with your hands to finish with your hands in the air. Your feet will have switched positions.

CARTWHEEL TO HANDSTAND ON WALL

1

Stand with side to the wall.

Keep the mat against the wall. Standing with your side to the wall, place your hands on the floor, turning them 90 degrees from your body, shoulder-width apart. Kick one leg up to the wall, followed quickly by the other leg. Your body should be stretched and tight. Hold for balance. Come down slowly the same way you went up.

2

Kick up to hand-stand position.

3

Lower legs back to start position.

FLOOR EXERCISE

KICK TO HANDSTAND

1 *Face the wall.*

2 *Kick to handstand position.*

Face the wall. It will not act as your support, but as a safety measure. Place your hands in front of your feet, shoulder-width apart. Kick one leg to a handstand, the other leg following quickly. Keep your body stretched, avoiding an arched back. Keep your head neutral, hands on the ground and your eyes looking at the floor. Hold this position for strength and balance, then step slowly down to the floor. When you are comfortable with this progression, move away from the wall completely. Your coach will stand nearby to shadow.

Cartwheels

This is one of the most popular and basic moves in gymnastics.

HAND-TO-HAND-FOOT-FOOT

1 Start position.

2 Hands are on rope, one leg in the air.

3 Legs kick to the other side of the rope.

4 Lunge to finish.

Let's look at the basic elements of a cartwheel. Place a rope in a circle on the floor. In a start position, face the inside of the circle. Moving to the side, place one hand on the rope, followed by the other hand. Kick your leg around, followed closely by the other leg to swivel around the rope. Finish in a lunge.

FLOOR EXERCISE

CARTWHEEL OVER ROPE AND PYLONS

1

Start position.

Now do a cartwheel over rope and pylons. This will force you to lift your feet a little higher over a few obstacles.

2

Both hands between ropes.

3

Lunge position.

CARTWHEEL OVER BLOCK

Now move to an elevated block. This will force you to lift your feet even higher, and kick harder. Place one foot in front of the other on the floor. Place your hands on the block, turning them 90 degrees from your body. In a cartwheel action, kick over the block to the other side, landing in a lunge. Repeat this movement on either side of the block.

FLOOR EXERCISE

CARTWHEEL ON THE FLOOR

1 *Starting position.*

2 *Kick over through handstand position.*

3 *Follow through to landing.*

4 *Lunge position.*

Having completed all these progressions, now try your full cartwheel on the floor. Pass through the handstand position and finish in a lunge.

ONE-ARMED CARTWHEEL

This is the more challenging cartwheel move. This skill starts off like a regular cartwheel but it is important to note that the opposite hand, or second hand, will be the supporting arm on the floor.

FLOOR EXERCISE

ROUND OFF

1

Mid-air, showing the push-off of the hands.

2

The landing.

Once you're confident with your cartwheel ability, the next challenging skill is the round off. The round off needs more power and upper body strength to complete.

This skill can be performed with a small run. Begin the same way as the regular cartwheel, but when your hands touch the floor you'll need more power, both from your legs kicking over, as well as the push from both hands, in order for your feet to land together, body upright.

THE BACK HANDSPRING

The back handspring is what's known as an aerial skill, which means that at one point, both your hands and your feet are not touching the ground. You'll be jumping backwards and the first thing to touch the ground will be your hands. Some young gymnasts find this daunting, so you need to be physically and emotionally ready. Discuss this skill with your coach.

We will demonstrate this skill with the use of a boulder mat. Stand facing away from the equipment, arms down by your side. Jump backwards with arms raised. You will land in a tight body position, stretched on top of the boulder. The boulder will tilt your body over to your hands. You will pass through a handstand position. Your legs will snap down as you push your arms up to a finish position. The boulder allows the coach and athlete to control the speed of the skill.

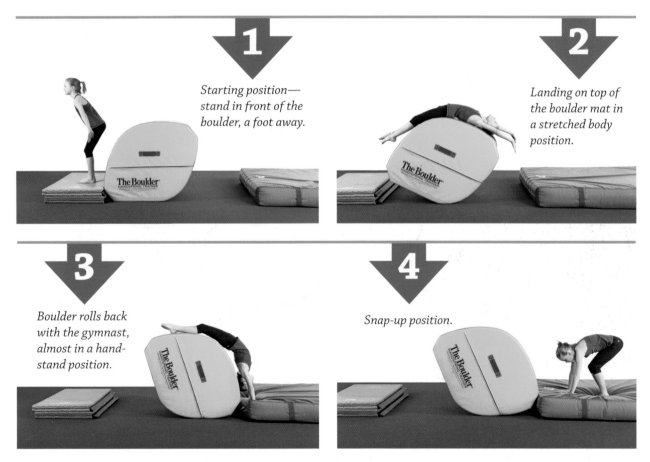

1 *Starting position— stand in front of the boulder, a foot away.*

2 *Landing on top of the boulder mat in a stretched body position.*

3 *Boulder rolls back with the gymnast, almost in a hand- stand position.*

4 *Snap-up position.*

Once you master this skill on the boulder, your coach will decide when you can remove the boulder mat and move to another surface.

VAULT

When learning vaulting skills for the first time, a trapezoid-shaped vault made with multi-level blocks is ideal.

RUN

Run toward the vault to gather acceleration and power.

HURDLE

Run toward the board, place one foot before the board, and jump with both feet on top of the board.

PREFLIGHT

Preflight is the position your body assumes when leaving the board, before touching the vault. You're airborne.

HANDS

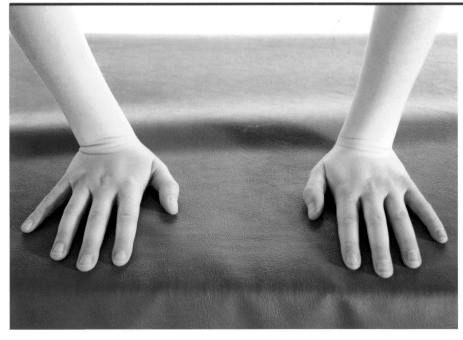

It's important to place your hands properly on top of the vault. Point your fingers forward, ensuring that your hands are flat on the vault, shoulder-width apart. Your hands should be slightly in front of your shoulders.

VAULT

Vaulting Skills

COURAGE VAULT

One of the first types of vaulting skills you'll learn is the Courage Vault. It's called the Courage Vault because it helps with your confidence, jumping from the board up onto the vault apparatus.

Jump from the board, place your hands onto the vault and tuck both knees up to your chest, placing them on top of the vault.

SQUAT ON VAULT

Jump off the board, place your hands shoulder-width apart on the vault, tuck your knees up to your chest and place your feet between your hands on top of the vault.

STRADDLE ON VAULT

Jump off the board, place your hands shoulder-width apart on the vault,
straddle your legs and place your feet on either side of your hands with
straight knees.

VAULT

Over the Vault

Once you feel comfortable performing these skills on the vault, it's time to progress and move over the apparatus.

SQUAT OVER

Jump off the board, place your hands on the vault shoulder-width apart and tuck your knees up to your chest, lifting your heels up and forward. Your legs will pass through your hands. Your shoulders should be slightly in front of your hands and your head should face forward. Use both hands to push off the vault. Land in a strong landing position.

STRADDLE OVER

Straddle over.

Brakes.

Jump off the board, place your hands on the vault shoulder-width apart and straddle your straight legs, lifting your heels up and forward. Your shoulders should be slightly in front of your hands, and your head should face forward. Use both hands to push off the vault, and then bring your feet together to absorb the landing.

FRONT HANDSPRING VAULT PROGRESSION

Placing hands onto the mat, push off hands, passing through a handstand position.

Landing on top of the boulder, on your back, in a stretched body position.

Boulder tilts gymnast to an upright standing position.

We will demonstrate a progression for a front handspring vault with the aid of the boulder mat. Place your hands on the mat. Push off your hands, passing through a handstand position to land stretched out on top of the boulder mat. The boulder will tilt to help you land, standing onto your feet. Discuss trying the actual front handspring vault with your coach, who will need to be present to help you follow through safely.

BARS

A variety of bars can be used for recreational purposes: the single bar (or high bar), parallel bars, uneven bars and even the rings.

Basic Grip Positions

Here are a few hand positions to practice when learning new skills on bars.

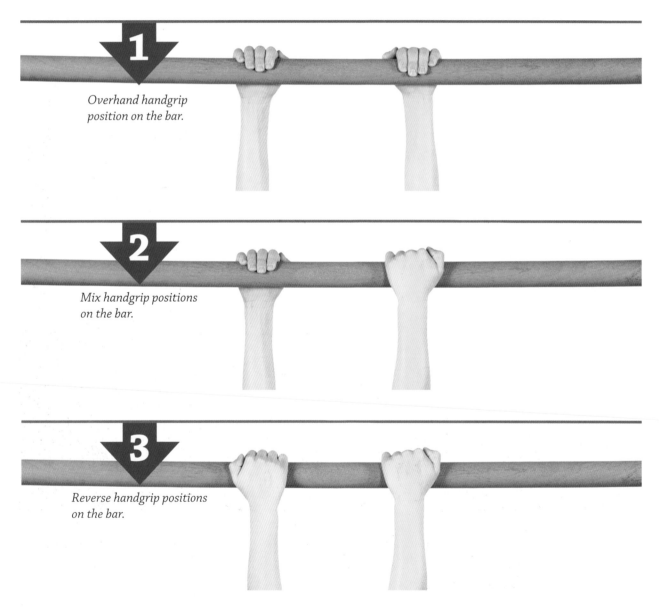

Overhand handgrip position on the bar.

Mix handgrip positions on the bar.

Reverse handgrip positions on the bar.

Hangs

Hangs are static, or still, positions during which the shoulders are below the bar.

TUCK HANG

PIKE HANG

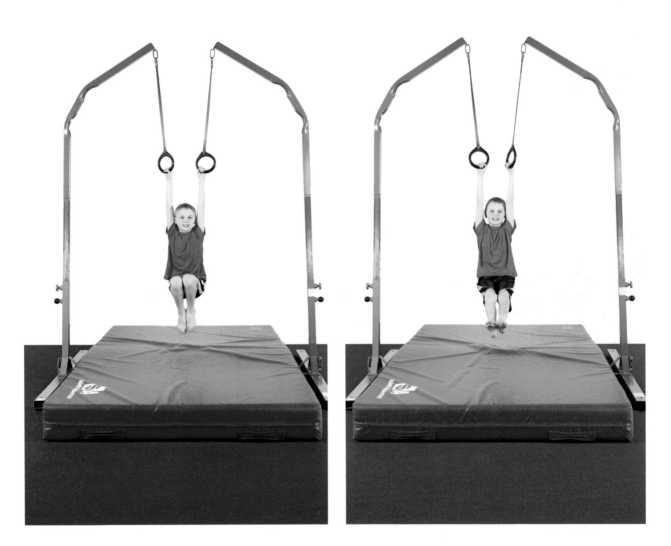

Reach up to the bar (or rings), hold on with both hands, maintain straight arms and lift both your legs into a tuck position.

Reach up to the bar (or rings) and extend your legs from the hips in an L position.

BARS

STRADDLE HANG

SOLE HANG

Stretch out your legs like a star.

Hold the bar with straight arms, lift both legs up toward the bar and place your feet on the bar on either side of your hands. Keep your legs straight and your chin pulled in to your chest.

Supports

A support is a static position that is performed with your shoulders above the bar.

FRONT SUPPORT ON UNEVEN BARS

This is one of the most important positions on bars for beginning and ending elements. To move into position, jump up to the bar with your body and arms straight. Push downward through your arms to raise your body, with your shoulders slightly in front of your hands. Ensure that the bar rests across your hips, not your stomach.

BARS

CROSS SUPPORT

Put one hand on each of the parallel bars, shoulders above your hands, in a hold, with your legs stretched (variations are tuck and pike positions).

Swings

Swings are an integral part of gymnastics on the bars. To swing safely, you must have a good understanding of hangs and supports.

GLIDE SWING

You can learn this swing by standing on top of a block. Hold onto the bar, with your body slightly bent at the hips. Lift both feet off the block. Your body will be in a stretched position at the middle of the swing. Swing back to your start position, keeping your feet in front of your body.

BARS

Strength Elements

It's important to practice strength moves to improve your overall gymnastic performance. You must be able to hold your body weight in order to progress. Here are some examples of strength elements.

CHIN UP

Pull your body up to the single bar so that your chin is above the bar and not resting on top. Hold for 3 to 5 seconds. Try the different handgrip positions (see page 54).

PULL UP

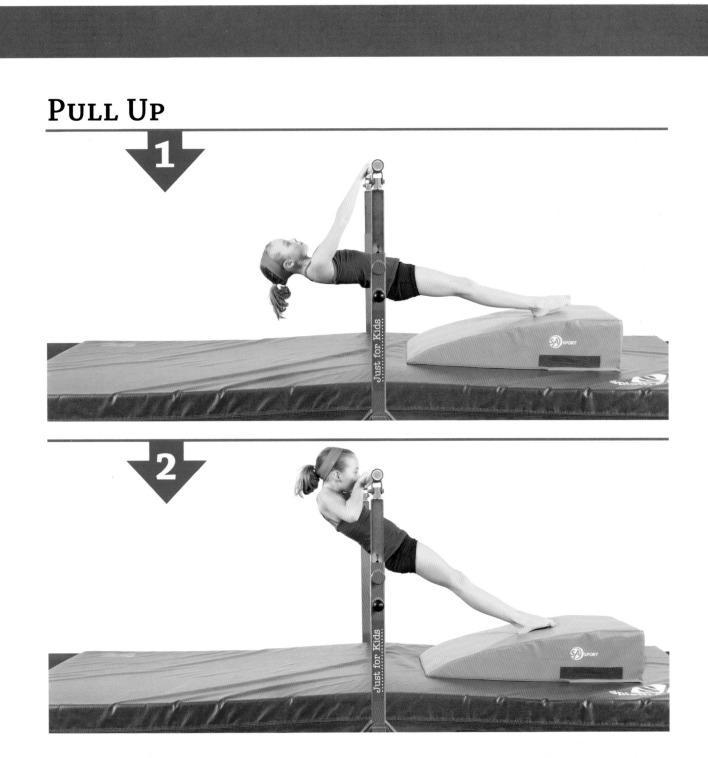

Hold onto the bar with your body in a stretched position, arms straight. Pull your upper body to the bar. It should look like you're performing an upside-down push-up.

BARS

BENT-ARM HOLD

Working with a set of rings, keep them still, while bending your elbows into your body, and pull your entire body up to the rings. Tuck your knees into your chest and hold. A variation on this move is called an L-hold position, in which your legs are extended straight out from your body.

ROPE CLIMBING

The rope-climbing station is an excellent addition to a recreational program to increase strength and awareness of height.

BARS

Rotations

Rotation is the movement of your body around itself or an apparatus.

FORWARD ROLL DOWN

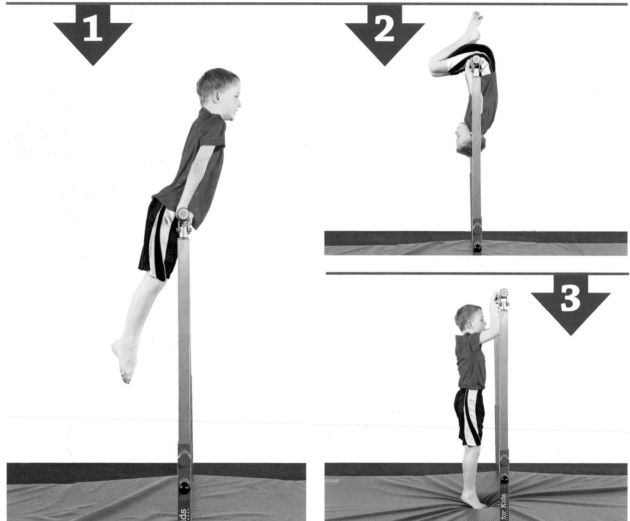

From a front support position, begin to lean your body forward by tucking your chin into your chest and bending at your waist. Rotate slowly around the bar, keeping your body in a tucked position. Continue the forward roll action around the bar until you end in a standing position on the floor.

HIP PULLOVER

1

Chin-up, one leg kicking, one foot on the wedge.

2

Gymnast circling around the bar.

3

Finish in the front support position.

4

For a challenge, take this to the high bar.

Holding onto the bar, perform a chin-up, kicking your legs up and over, bending at your hips to sandwich the bar between your upper and lower body. Continue the circle, allowing your hands to slide around the bar, and finish in a front support position.

BARS

CASTING

From a front support position, lean slightly forward with
your shoulders, sandwiching the bar with your hips. Push
your hips away from the bar with straight arms, maintaining
a straight body. Your hips should return to the bar.

BACKWARD HIP CIRCLE

From a front support position, lean slightly forward with your shoulders, bending in with your hips. Cast your body and allow your hips to return to the bar like a magnet to complete the full 360-degree rotation. As your body rotates backward, tuck your chin into your chest. Your hands should move freely around the bar. End in a front support.

BARS

STRADDLE ON MOUNT

Stand with your hands on the low bar, feet on the board. Jump up to the bar with your shoulders leaning forward over your hands. Your feet will leave the board in order to land on the low bar in a straddle position. When you feel balanced, lift your arms up to grab the high bar. A variation is doing this mount in the squat position.

DISMOUNT

1

Cast away.

2

Land.

Use the front support position, cast, and push off the bar. Release the bar to land in a brakes position on the floor. It's an important skill to know how to dismount safely off the apparatus, especially at this height. Most importantly, don't forget to let go!

BALANCE BEAM

In a recreational setting, it is best to use a low balance beam when starting out. This helps gymnasts gain confidence while learning new skills. At our gym, we often add an extender to our high beam, which widens the beam and adds confidence during practice.

Mounts and Dismounts

Mounts and dismounts are ways of getting on and off the apparatus.

Mounts

STRADDLE MOUNT

Stand facing the side of the beam. Place your hands on the beam, shoulder-width apart, and jump onto the beam, landing in a straddle position with your shoulders slightly in front of your hands.

SQUAT MOUNT

Place your hands shoulder-width apart on the beam, jump from the floor, tuck your knees up to your chest and place your feet between your hands on top of the beam.

WOLF MOUNT

Stand facing the side of the beam. Place your hands on top of the beam and jump up, bringing one leg up in a tucked position and placing that foot on the beam, between your hands. Bring your other leg up on top of the beam, outside your hands, and extend it. Try to do these two moves simultaneously. Your arms can remain on top of the beam or you can extend them outward.

BALANCE BEAM

JUMP UP MOUNT

Run and hurdle onto the board. Jump in a straight body position onto the balance beam.

Dismounts

TUCK JUMP DISMOUNT

Stand on the beam. Jump to a tuck position in the air from the end or side of the beam, lifting your arms over your head. At the top of the jump, place your hands on top of your knees before landing on two feet, with your arms to the side. Bend your knees to absorb the landing.

STRADDLE JUMP DISMOUNT

Stand on the beam. Jump up in the air, straddling your legs to the side, and bring your legs back together, absorbing the landing on the mat.

BALANCE BEAM

JUMP DISMOUNT WITH ROTATIONS

Jump half turn in air.

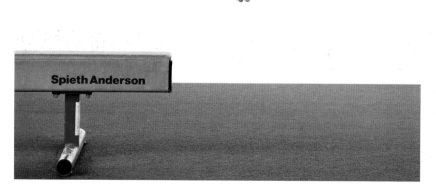

Stand on the beam. Jump off and make a half-turn with your arms in the air and with a straight body, absorbing the landing on the mat. You can eventually progress to a full turn, also known as a "360."

ROUND-OFF DISMOUNT

This is the more challenging dismount and should be discussed with your coach. Place your hands at the end of the beam, kick your legs over your head through the handstand position, push off the beam with your hands, and land on the mat upright.

BALANCE BEAM

Complex

This is a variety of progressive-type warm-up movements used to ready the body for balance and steadiness on the beam. Begin by walking forward, backward and sideward on the beam. Then progress to walking on your toes.

WALK FORWARD

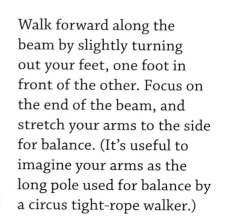

Walk forward along the beam by slightly turning out your feet, one foot in front of the other. Focus on the end of the beam, and stretch your arms to the side for balance. (It's useful to imagine your arms as the long pole used for balance by a circus tight-rope walker.)

WALK BACKWARD

Walk backwards by placing one foot behind the other. Again, focus on the end of the beam. Feel the side of the beam as you place your foot behind, keeping your arms to your sides and your head neutral.

WALK SIDEWARD

Facing the side of the beam, step one foot to the side and close the other foot to it. Continue moving in the same direction until you've reached the end of the beam. Keep your head neutral and focus on the beam mats in front of you.

CROSSOVER WALK (OR GRAPEVINE WALK)

Place one foot in front of the other, continue in the same direction, stepping with your opposite leg. Continue the motion sideward down the beam, with your legs crossing over forward or crossing behind.

BALANCE BEAM

DIP WALK

Walk forward by slightly bending one knee and dipping the other foot down along the side of the beam. Then bring that same foot up on top of the beam in front of the support foot.

LUNGE STEP

Step forward on one foot, bending your knee while your back knee rests on the beam. Your front knee will be directly over your front foot, with your arms stretched out to the side. Stand up and step forward with the back foot, repeating the lunge, arms to the side.

Stationary Positions

Stationary positions are "held" or "still" positions. Many stationary positions require good balance.

STORK STAND

Stand on the beam, arms stretched out to the side for balance. Raise one foot up to the knee of your support leg by bending at the knee of your working leg. Hold this position for a few seconds. Switch legs.

FRONT SCALE

From a standing position, lift one leg behind you. Lower your upper body as your leg lifts in the air. Keep both legs straight, arms to the side for balance, and keep your head neutral.

BALANCE BEAM

KNEE SCALE

From a lunge step position (see page 78), allow your front knee to rest on the beam while your arms support your upper body. Extend your back leg.

V SIT

While sitting on the beam, place your hands on the beam, behind your hips, and raise your legs in front of your body into a V position.

Leaps

Leaps are a dance-type element used on balance beam.

SCISSOR LEAP

From a stand with one leg forward, step onto one leg while your back leg swings forward to a kick. Switch your legs in the air and land in a stand on the first kick foot.

Balance Beam

Jumps

Stretched Jump

1 Push off, arms extended.

2 Tuck.

3 Pike.

Stand with one foot in front of the other. Push off of both feet and stretch your body in the air, with your arms extending up. Land with both feet on the beam. This is a fairly basic jump and can be performed in various positions: tuck, pike, straddle and turning jumps, including rotations of 90, 180 and 360 degrees.

Turns

PIVOT TURN

1
Rise up onto the balls of the feet.

2
Turn 180 degrees.

3
Finish facing the other end of the beam.

Stand on the beam, facing the end with one foot in front of the other. Rise up onto the balls of your feet and turn 180 degrees toward your back foot to face the other end of the beam.

BALANCE BEAM

FORWARD KICK TURN

1 *Lift one leg in front.*

2 *Turn, finishing with leg behind body.*

Lift one leg in front and perform a half-turn on the other foot. Finish with your leg up behind your body, keeping your arms to the side for balance.

FORWARD ROLL

From a start position, squat down on the beam, with your hands reaching forward on the beam. Tuck your head down, chin to chest, push off your legs and roll over onto your back. Finish in a standing position on the beam.

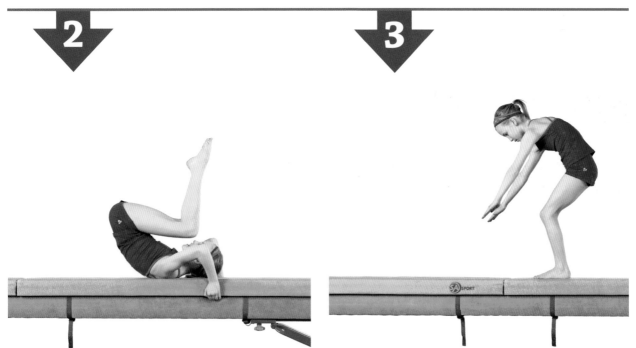

BALANCE BEAM

CARTWHEEL

1

Cartwheel on the high beam.

2

Stand on the beam with one foot in front, arms raised. Place your hands on the beam while your back leg kicks over and through a handstand position. Your back leg lands first, followed by your front leg...

CARTWHEEL CONTINUED

Lunge finish.

... finishing in a lunge position.

CHAPTER 7

Cooling Down

Cooling down is just as important as warming up. During your workout, your muscles will produce lactic acid. Cooling down helps the body return to a normal state.

Cool downs are usually 15 minutes long, starting with a fun group activity that recaps the skills learned during that class. At our gym, we might do a freeze dance to music. Run around, and when the music stops, freeze in one of the skills you learned that day. Then the music starts again. You can play the same activity, making a letter of the alphabet with your body, or demonstrating a stationary skill, every time your coach yells freeze.

STRETCHING

Your final minutes in class can include any of the stretches done in the warm-up, with a few more options to keep it interesting. Here are a few new stretches to try:

GASTROCNEMIUS STRETCH

SOLEUS STRETCH

This exercise will stretch out your calf muscles. Stand facing a wall. Place one leg in front of the other, your front leg slightly bent at the knee, your back leg straight. Point your toes toward the wall. Place your hands on the wall and, keeping your back heel on the floor, lean forward to feel the stretch in your calf. Hold this stretch for 30 seconds and then switch legs.

The soleus is part of the calf muscle, underneath the gastrocnemius and connected to the Achilles tendon. Position your body as you did for the gastrocnemius stretch, but this time bend your back knee into your front knee, keeping your back heel on the floor. You will feel this stretch much lower in the leg. Hold for at least 30 seconds, stretching as far as you feel comfortable.

Rock 'N' Roll Stretch

Sit in a tuck position and roll backward and forward like a ball. Don't let your head touch the floor.

It's good to end your workout with a stretch to prevent stiffness or achiness the next day. And congratulate yourself: you did something fun and great for your body.

All in all, the best part about finishing today's gymnastics class is being excited about the next one.

CHAPTER 8

Adding Rhythm and Bounce To Your Program

Any great recreational program can take the sport of gymnastics to another level by enhancing the experience with elements like trampoline, and rhythmic activities.

Rhythmic Gymnastics

Rhythmic gymnastics is a fun way to incorporate coordination and creativity into a recreational program. It develops both sides of the body, promotes eye-hand coordination, and is excellent for strengthening. Using "playground" apparatuses like rope, hoop, ball, ribbon and clubs, you'll develop basic skills such as bouncing, throwing, catching and rotating, while incorporating simple gymnastics and dance-type elements. It can be acrobatic too, and music can be used to create rhythmical combinations.

You can compete in rhythmic gymnastics either as an individual or in a group (which can be very fun). You may discover that you're happier doing a team sport; if so, group rhythmic gymnastics is an excellent option for you.

Before beginning with the apparatus, there are a few things to consider about rhythmic gymnastics. There are specific individual skills that you can learn with all these apparatuses, and when the skills are mastered, you can add dance elements, leaps, turns and jumps and many of these skills in combination with others. It is also fun to try these skills with both hands. You will discover that one side of your body is easier to command than the other side. Rhythmic gymnasts have the challenge of moving their body and moving the apparatus at the same time, while making it look easy and elegant.

Before we begin, you may wonder where you can buy rhythmic equipment. Consult with staff at your gym—your coach will be able to help you find a distributor of rhythmic equipment, designed for Recreational through to Elite. Practice at your gym with all the equipment until you know how to use the pieces correctly. Then… get rhythmic!

ROPE

It's important to find a rope that is the right length for your frame. When you hold the rope at the ends and stand in the middle with your feet shoulder width apart, the ends of the rope should reach your underarms.

Basic skills with rope include skipping, swings, rotations (or circles), tosses and catches.

Skipping with the rope is not only great exercise but can be done in many different ways. Skipping can be done forward, backward and sideward. You can add crossover skipping and double skips. Skipping can also be completed by moving across the floor.

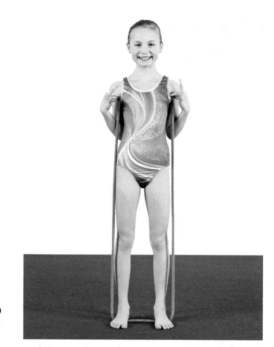

SWINGS

Swinging the rope can be a challenge because the rope should always look taught (like the letter "U") and never like a wet noodle. You can swing the rope with both ends in one hand, or one end in each hand. Swings can occur in front of the body, to the side and behind your body.

CIRCLES

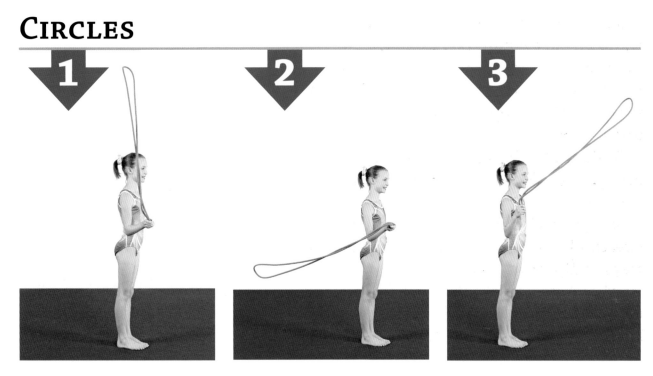

Doing circles, otherwise known as rotations, is another skill. Many rhythmic gymnasts pretend they are helicopters or cowgirls when they do rotations. Rotations can be practiced over the head, under the legs, and to the side.

TOSSES AND CATCHES

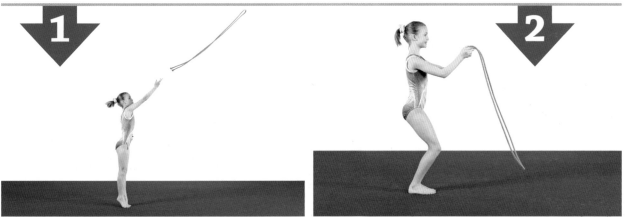

When you have mastered skipping and rotations, you can start tossing the rope and catching. It is fun to watch the rope rotate in the air while completing a dance or gymnastics move and catching the rope, all within a few seconds!

HOOP

The "hula dance," where you keep the hoop circling around the middle of your body, is usually the first move everyone loves to do when they pick up a hula-hoop. Rhythmic gymnasts are no different. They love to do the hula as well. The basic skills you can learn with the hoop include swings and circles, rolls, rotations, and throws and catches.

SWINGS & CIRCLES

ROLLS

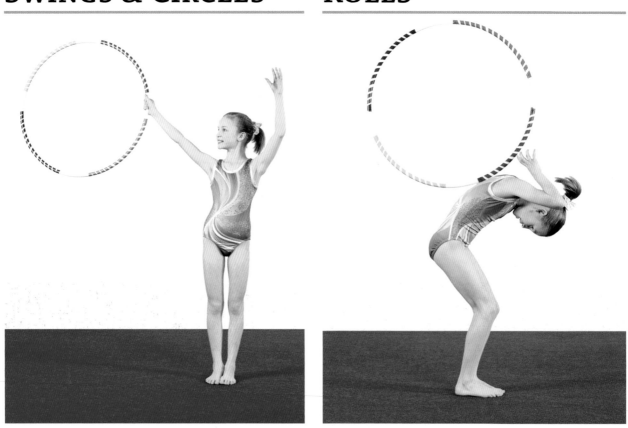

Swings and circles can be done with a hoop, much in the same way they are done with a rope. Swing and circle the hoop in front of your body, on the side, and also while jumping through the hoop. Circles are especially fun when you move the hoop over and under your body. Skipping is a full circle with the hoop.

You can roll the hoop on the floor and also on your body. You can roll the hoop to a partner in all types of directions. Rolls on the body are especially fun. The hoop can be rolled across one arm, over your shoulders and neck, all the way across your other arm.

ROTATIONS

THROWS & CATCHES

Rotations with the hoop are mostly completed on your hand, but can also be done on your ankle. When you rotate the hoop in your hand, rotate it between your thumb and fingers with your thumb pointing upward. This will give you the most control. Have some fun switching hands while rotating. You can also rotate over your head and to the side.

Throws and catches are especially fun. From a rotation skill, toss the hoop in the air, spin it, and catch it again. A more challenging move is to perform a flip toss (pancake toss) and catch while skipping. Take throws to the next level by adding forward rolls and cartwheels.

BALL

With the ball, you can learn several skills, including swings, rolls, bounces, throws and catches.

A rhythmic ball is not a basketball: you won't be juggling or dribbling with it. Keep your arms stretched out, and hold the ball, relaxing your hand and spreading out your fingers.

Now, start swinging your arm forward and backward to the side of

your body, keeping the ball pointing up. We coach gymnasts to point the "belly button" of the ball (where the ball gets pumped up) to the sky and keep it there while swinging the ball.

You can roll the ball either on your body or on the floor. You can follow it with leaps and dance elements, and you can even roll your body on it.

Rolling the ball on one arm at a time is another challenge. A good way to practice "feeling" the ball on your arm is to extend your arm out with the palm of your hand, facing upward. Place the ball in between your wrist and your elbow. Let go of the ball and see how long you can balance the ball on your arm. You can also try that with two balls at the same time.

At the 2007 Special Olympics in Beijing, Emily Boycott was the winner of 5 gold medals in Rope, Ribbon, Hoop, Ball and also All-Around. She has been on the Canadian Special Olympics team twice, in China and in Athens.

BOUNCING

THROWS & CATCHES

Bouncing the ball can be done with two hands, one hand and alternating hands. Keep your chest up and push the ball down each time you bounce it. The ball can also be bounced off of different body parts such as your chest, knee, elbow, shoulder and even your head.

After you have learned to swing the ball, you can toss it in the air and catch it with one hand or both hands. When you catch the ball, catch it with your hand up high and "absorb" the catch with your hand and arm so the ball does not "slap" in your hand. It is also fun to catch the ball with different body parts, such as under your legs. This is called a trap catch.

RIBBON

A rhythmic gymnast competes with a ribbon that is 6 meters (about 19.5 feet) in length. A 4-meter ribbon (about 13 feet) is the best size to use in a recreational program.

The ribbon is a favorite apparatus in rhythmic gymnastics because it is so beautiful to watch. The ribbon catches everybody's attention right away. When you try activities with the ribbon, try to keep the entire ribbon moving at all times.

Before you start with the ribbon, you need to learn the proper way to hold the stick. This is important to help you make the best possible patterns. Place the bottom of the stick in the middle of the palm of your hand. Grasp the stick with your hand and place your index finger along the stick.

You can think about the ribbon and the stick as a brush, painting a picture in the air. Or pretend to draw your name in cursive with the ribbon in the air.

Sometimes the ribbon may get tangled and form a knot. This can happen when the ribbon is too close to the body or if the entire ribbon is not moving. Don't get frustrated though, it happens to the best rhythmic gymnasts!

Some of the skills you can learn with ribbon are large circles, spirals and snakes.

LARGE CIRCLES

Use your entire arm to lift the whole ribbon off the floor, forming large circles in the air. These circles can be completed over your head, in front and beside your body.

SPIRALS

These patterns are very tight and small. You can do spirals in front, beside and behind your body. It is important to remember to keep the stick pointing downward so the ribbon does not get tangled. These circular movements are performed successfully when your wrist circles quickly. Your arm may get a little tired, so switch hands to give your first arm a rest.

SNAKES

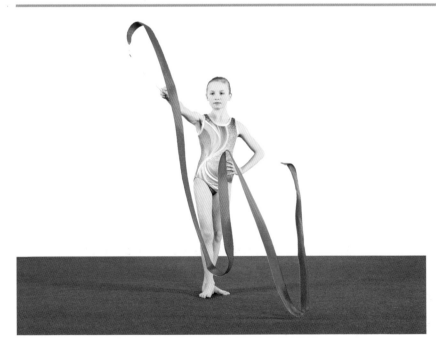

Snake actions are initiated by the wrist in a side-to-side movement. They can be completed in front or beside your body, as well as over your head. You can compare snakes to scribbling in the air. It can be fun to make snake sounds while doing this pattern.

CLUBS

Clubs are an apparatus that are made of hard plastic and are unevenly weighted on each end. They look similar to bowling pins. Clubs are used in competitive rhythmic gymnastics but may not be used in all recreational gym environments because they can be challenging. Practice with softer apparatus like scarves, balls inside socks, or even rubber chickens. Eventually, if you're successful with two soft props, try the clubs. They can be found in different sizes for all gymnasts.

When using clubs, you can learn swings, circles, tosses and catches.

SWINGS

Holding one or two clubs, swing them forward, backward and in front of your body. Think of your clubs as extensions of your arms, so that your arms look as long as possible.

CIRCLES

Circles include "mills." Hold the bottom of the club between your thumb and middle finger. Circle the clubs by rotating your wrist. You can do this move in front of your body and to the side. Clubs can also be circled using your shoulder forward and backward.

TOSSES & CATCHES

Clubs can be tossed very low and really high. It is exciting to watch competitive rhythmic gymnasts toss the clubs high in the air while completing multiple rolls, leaps and jumps before catching the clubs. When you toss the clubs low, you can flip them quickly in your hand. It is fun to catch the clubs with other body parts as well, including your legs, behind your knees, in the crook of your arm or even in your armpit.

Elfi's scrapbook

While growing up, I specialized in artistic gymnastics. When my sister Andrea was 11, she moved from artistic gymnastics into rhythmic. "Four Continents," an international gymnastics event, was held in Toronto in 1987. Andrea and her teammates were representing Canada, so it was an important day for her. This event also marked my debut as a rhythmic commentator: I was preparing to commentate the 1988 Olympic Games in Seoul, Korea. I was nervous about getting this first event under my belt. But I was also nervous because my sister was competing. I remember how proud I felt watching her team march out to the floor to begin their routine. I was captivated by their talent and synchronicity. Of course my eyes were on Andrea, and I could see how happy she was to participate in a sport that showed off her talents. When her team finished their routine, there was much celebration. After training so hard, they had performed spectacularly.

Andrea Schlegel was a member of the Canadian National Rhythmic Gymnastics team from 1984 to 1989, competing both as an individual and group member. Andrea represented Canada internationally in Hungary, the Czech Republic and the United States. She is now a National Coaching Certification Program (NCCP) Foundations of Gymnastics Facilitator for both artistic and rhythmic gymnastics.

TRAMPOLINE

The trampoline is a tremendous form of exercise—not to mention, a lot of fun! Everyone loves the feeling of jumping on the trampoline and being suspended in the air—it's like being on a roller coaster.

Did You Know?... In the 2000 Sydney Olympics, Canadian trampolinist Karen Cockburn won Bronze in trampoline. In both the 2004 Athens Olympics and the 2008 Beijing Olympics, she won Silver. She's the most successful male or female trampolinist Canada has ever produced.

Safety

Before starting, your coach will point out a few basic safety measures that must be respected.

- ✔ Only one person may use the trampoline at any time. Two people pose a risk of injury.
- ✔ The center is the safest place to jump on the trampoline.
- ✔ Hold your head neutral, eyes slightly down, focusing on the end of the trampoline.
- ✔ The safest way to land is with your weight equally distributed on both legs as they come into contact with the trampoline.
- ✔ It's important to know when to stop—also known as "putting on the brakes." Injuries can occur if you're jumping out of control.

Foot-to-Foot Skills

STRAIGHT JUMP

Stand still on the trampoline, without bouncing. Jump into the air, extending your arms up and forward, keeping your body in a straight line. Land on both feet, relaxing your knees. Now repeat with a low bounce.

TRAMPOLINE

TUCK JUMP

PIKE JUMP

STRADDLE JUMP

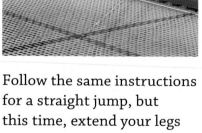

Follow the same instructions for the straight jump, but at the highest point of the jump, bring your knees up to your chest in a tuck position, with your hands touching the tops of your knees. Straighten your body before landing on the trampoline.

Jump up, bringing your legs up in front and extending them from the hips. Reach your arms forward, and touch the top of your feet with your fingers. Do not lean too far forward and keep your head neutral.

Follow the same instructions for a straight jump, but this time, extend your legs and arms out in a straddle position at the highest point of the jump.

TWISTING JUMPS

1

Twist shoulders and hips.

2

Landing.

The takeoff for twisting jumps is similar to straight jumps. Lift your body off the trampoline, with your arms in the air. This time, however, twist your shoulders and hips. To keep your balance, look straight ahead both before and after the twist. Start by doing a simple half-twist jump with no bounce. Add more bounce once you're comfortable. When you've mastered the half-twist, you can progress to a full twist.

TRAMPOLINE

SEAT DROP

Jump up, lifting your legs and extending them forward. Land in an L sitting position on the trampoline, with your hands on the trampoline, fingers pointing forward. Push your hands off the trampoline and finish in a stand. Begin this skill with no bounce and eventually progress to a low bounce.

SWIVEL HIP

This skill starts off like a seat drop, but requires more power to lift your body up in the air. After completing the seat drop, push your hands off the trampoline in order to generate greater lift. Rotate your body 180 degrees, turning in a straight line to complete another seat drop. The skill is finished when the skill is done twice.

HAND-AND-KNEE DROP

Squat down low to the trampoline, leaning your body forward. Jump down to your hands and knees, letting them land simultaneously on the trampoline. Keep your arms relaxed when hitting the trampoline bed. Your back should be level, with your head looking at a focal point at the end of the trampoline. When you are comfortable, eliminate the squat start, and begin from a standing position.

TRAMPOLINE

FRONT DROP

1

Hand-and-knee drop position.

2

Land in a front drop position.

Start from the hand-and-knee drop position on the trampoline. With a little push, extend your body and land in a front drop position. Your body should be completely stretched with your arms bent to your sides. Hold your head high enough to be able to see the end of the trampoline. When you become confident, begin from a standing position.

BACK DROP

1 *Start in a low squat position.*

2 *Land flat on back.*

From a low squat position, do a very small jump backwards from both feet. You should land flat onto your back, without your legs or head touching the trampoline. Your head and arms are up toward the ceiling.

Combinations

Once you've mastered these skills, you can challenge yourself to perform them in combination.

For example, you could perform:

- ✔ a tuck jump to a straddle jump to a straight jump
- ✔ a seat drop to a hand-and-knee drop, or vice versa
- ✔ a seat drop, to a hand-and-knee drop, to a front drop back to a hand-and-knee drop, and stand up.

The possibilities for mini-routines are endless. Practice often, be safe and have fun!

CHAPTER 9

Gymnastics' Greats from Yesterday to Today

Stealing the Limelight: A Look at the Greats

When gymnastics first became popular, athletes were often old enough to be married. But for the last forty years, gymnastics has been coined the "Cinderella sport" because female gymnasts are often the youngest athletes in competition. Audiences around the world marvel at how focused, motivated and disciplined these athletes are for their age. And with every new Olympics, a young gymnast manages to steal the limelight and become internationally known by her first name only. She is a star who transcends both borders and languages.

These are just a few of the gymnasts who have made a difference and pushed the boundaries of gymnastics.

Mary Lou Retton catapulted to international fame by winning the All-Around Gold Medal in women's gymnastics at the 1984 Olympic Games in Los Angeles, becoming the first American woman ever to win a gold medal in gymnastics.

Olga Korbut

Olga Korbut at the 1976 Montreal Olympics.

Nadia Comaneci

Nadia Comaneci on balance beam at the 1979 World Cup Gymnastics Championship.

Mary Lou Retton

Mary Lou Retton, the gold medalist from the 1984 Los Angeles Olympics.

Elfi's scrapbook

At the 1984 Olympics in Los Angeles, California, Mary Lou Retton became the first American gymnast to win an Olympic gold medal. Her coach was Bela Karolyi, the same coach who made Nadia Comaneci a champion. Although Mary Lou wasn't the favorite to win, she thrived on pressure. She had incredible strength and determination. Her bubbly, infectious personality made people marvel at her seemingly boundless energy. Winning the gold made her famous; she did commercials, made "celebrity" appearances and even ended up on a Wheaties cereal box!

Vitaly Scherbo

Elfi's scrapbook

In Barcelona in 1992, Belorussian Vitaly Scherbo became the first male gymnast to win 6 gold medals. He won more medals than any athlete at that Olympics—in fact, more golds than any gymnast in a single Olympics.

Vitaly Scherbo performing on the pommel horse.

Kyle Shewfelt

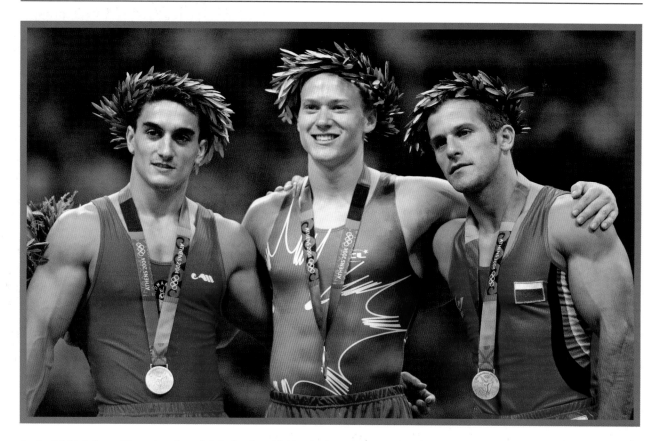

At the 2004 Athens Olympics, Canada's Kyle Shewfelt (middle) won the gold medal in the Men's Floor Exercise. Shewfelt is the most successful gymnast Canada has ever produced. He is the only Olympic Gold Medalist (2004, Athens), male or female, from Canada to date.

Kyle:

"I began gymnastics in 1988 when I was 6 years old. I was doing cartwheels around the house, handstands against the wall, and flips on the bed. My mom was going crazy! A neighbor across the street did gymnastics, so one day I was invited along to a practice. That's when the 'magic' started.

I showed promise and talent from an early age. I remember being interviewed by a local Calgary TV reporter when I was 9 years old. By then I'd been in the sport 3 years. He asked what my dream was and I answered, 'to go to the Olympics and win.' Every day, I worked hard toward this dream and knew it would happen.

I trained at Altadore Gymnastics in Calgary. There, I watched and learned from Jennifer Wood, a former Canadian team member and 1992 Olympian. I watched her process of becoming an Olympian. I'd say she was my mentor. As for people I admired, it was the Russian male gymnasts. They were so artistic, always pointing their toes, and very stylish in the corners of the floor exercise mat.

What's hard about being a competitive gymnast is the monotony of the day-to-day training; doing the same thing over and over. I didn't mind trying to be perfect in my skills, but I didn't enjoy the sore body from all the training."

Q&A

Kyle's Most Challenging Skill:

"I remember when I was 16, Eugene Galperin, a Russian coach who lived in Canada, came out to Calgary to coach for 3 months. He wanted to teach me a skill called a 'Def'—it's a one-and-a-half twisting release skill on the high bar. I said no way! He kept saying, just try it. He was so clever in the way he got me to learn the skill. We started off one day just attempting it, but I couldn't have been further from the bar, with no hope of catching it. Eventually, after 3 months, I caught the move. So you can get it if you try."

Most Challenging Event:

"My most difficult event was the pommel horse—always very clunky for me. But even with difficult moves, if you try hard enough, you can do it."

Favorite Gymnastics Moments:

"One: The 2000 Olympics, and actually becoming an Olympian for the very first time. Two: Winning a gold medal at the 2004 Athens Olympics, and standing on the podium. I remember looking into the audience and seeing my coach of 16 years, Kelly Manjak, and my mom and dad. I remember all those fundraising bingo nights they had to go through to get me there. And three: Making a comeback after a long recovery from a serious injury, and actually making the Olympic team for the 2008 Beijing Olympics."

What Kyle Loves About the Sport:

"Learning a new skill, inventing something new, the creativity of it all… and chasing your dreams."

Elfi's scrapbook

I followed Kyle's career over the years, watching him grow as an international athlete, working his way to the top. Kyle built his reputation on being different, innovative and polished. I was commentating at the 2004 Athens Olympics for NBC Sports, and watched Kyle perform in the floor exercise. It was no surprise to me that he captured the gold medal. The pride I felt as a Canadian was overwhelming. I knew Kyle had accomplished something great: the first Canadian to ever win an Olympic Gold medal in gymnastics!

Did You Know?… At the 2000 Olympics, Kyle performed a brand new vault. The new move was ratified by the judges, and thereafter it was called The Shewfelt Vault.

Tim Daggett

1984 Olympic Gold Medalist, USA. Tim Daggett scored a perfect 10 that clinched the Gold for the USA Men's Team on High Bar. He also won an individual Bronze on pommel horse.

Tim:

"My first encounter with gymnastics was pure coincidence. I was involved in another high school sport and was heading down the hall for a drink when I peered through the gym door window. I saw a guy swinging on a bar that was about 10 feet high in the air. He picked up speed every time (later I'd learn he was doing 'giants') and finally let go. His body flew about 13 feet high in the air, did a back flip and then, with no effort at all, he landed on two feet. Wow! I couldn't believe it.

So I began to compete. I never felt like I was missing out on anything—I loved the sport and for 17 years, it was my best friend. It was the first thing I thought of when I woke up and the last thing I thought about before falling asleep. It was who I was."

118

Spotlight on Today's Gymnastic Stars

I talked to several of today's elite gymnasts to get the inside scoop on their exciting lives as competitive athletes.

Emily Boycott

Emily:

"I took gymnastics when I was a little girl and liked it very much. I got into rhythmic gymnastics when I was 16 because my mom heard about it from a friend. I like music and dance, so it was a great fit. When we started rhythmic gymnastics, my mom was just learning about the sport, so Andrea Schlegel at Schlegel's Gymnastics Centre in Oakville helped us out. Andrea is so kind and generous. She knows a lot about rhythmic gymnastics and she believed in me. She is my choreographer.

I admire Alexandra Orlando and Carly Orava, who competed for Canada. They are very talented. They are flexible and have very pointed toes. Mary Sanders competed for the United States in rhythmic gymnastics. Mary and I did a dance together called 'Rise Up' at a Special Olympics Gala in Toronto. When I nail a routine, it really makes me feel good."

At the 2007 Special Olympics in Beijing, Emily Boycott was the winner of 5 gold medals in Rope, Ribbon, Hoop, Ball and also All-Around. She has been on the Canadian Special Olympics team twice, in China and in Athens.

Q&A

Most Challenging Skill:

"My most challenging skill is the horizontal turn. Sometimes I get it and sometimes I don't."

Funny Gymnastics Moment:

"Once, I was lined up to compete, but I sat down in the hall and fell asleep. They called me to go and I was still sleepy and I got my routine all mixed up."

Goals and Dreams:

"This year we start our Special Olympics cycle all over. It takes 4 years, starting with our provincial qualifier. I am learning some new routines and some new moves so I don't get bored. I want to go to Nationals and the World Games. I will have to train, do my workouts, and work hard to qualify for Worlds. I love being with my friends, traveling, meeting new people and just having a great time. I have been to China and Greece because of rhythmic gymnastics. When I am not flexible anymore, I want to be a coach."

Shallon Olsen

Shallon:

"My mother enrolled me in recreational gymnastics at the YMCA when I was 3 years old. I'm told I had lots of energy and my mom thought gymnastics would be a good fit for me.

Then, one day, my brother attended a birthday party at Omega Gymnastics Academy. When we started looking for a proper gymnastics club, my father checked Omega's website and discovered that most of the coaches were Russians. He liked this, knowing that Russians have traditionally been very strong in gymnastics. So my parents enrolled me at Omega.

I didn't really know much about well-known gymnasts when I started competing. However, Gael Mackie was training at our gym (and had been for more than a decade) and was just getting ready to attend the University of Utah. Gael had competed at the 2004 Summer Olympics in Athens, Greece. At her going-away party, she signed a bunch of photos of herself. On mine she wrote, 'Never give up on your dreams.' I have held onto those words whenever I have faced challenges in gymnastics. Gael has since finished her scholarship and is now working as a gymnastics coach. I admire her for her commitment to the sport and her perseverance. She is a good role model for young gymnasts.

I really admire Jordyn Wieber because she is a good gymnast. I also like Aliya Mustafina because she is consistent and strong. Both girls are mentally very tough. Of course, Nastia Liukin is great to watch because she has taken a lot of ballet. Shawn Johnson is a powerhouse, very strong and impressive. I admire that she's making a comeback after almost 4 years of no gymnastics."

Q&A

Goals and Dreams:

"My goal is to continue with gymnastics until I am old enough to go to the Olympics in 2016. After that I would like to go to school on a NCAA scholarship in the States. My dream is to not only compete at the Olympics, but to win some medals for Canada."

Shallon's Most Challenging Skill or Event:

"My most challenging skill is the Jaeger. Vault is my most challenging event."

A Great Memory:

"I have very good memories of going to the 2011 Canada Winter Games in Halifax, Nova Scotia. I thought it was just like the Olympics, going to the opening ceremonies and experiencing such excitement. I liked the cafeteria at the Athletes' Village and all the great food they served. I

At the 2011 Canadian National Championships, Shallon Olsen from Surrey, British Columbia, was first overall in the novice division.

also enjoyed playing the Wii and XBox 360 Kinect there."

A Funny Competitive Moment:

"I was on the beam and I could feel my bodysuit riding up. I felt that, if I didn't adjust it, I would fall on my next skill, so I pulled a wedgie. When I finished my routine, my coach scolded me because it was a deduction. She then imitated me pulling a wedgie and tugging at my bodysuit in an exaggerated way. The cameraman filmed the whole thing—it was embarrassing!"

Shawn Johnson

Q&A

Most memorable gymnastic moment:
"My most memorable moment would have to be the All-Around competition at the 2008 Beijing Olympic games. It was the the defining moment of my career. I competed with everything I had and have no regrets. It was the best moment of my life."

Most challenging thing about gymnastics:
"Finding the strength within yourself to do the impossible. Gymnasts are pushed harder than anyone and are normally under the age of 16! Mentally and physically, it takes so much. It's about finding that passion inside of you at such a young age, and competing as one of the best in the world, with the whole world watching."

American gymnast Shawn Johnson was named most famous living sports figure in her state of Iowa in 2010 after a career highlighted by back-to-back national titles in 2007 and 2008, the 2007 World All-Around Champion, and an Olympic Gold Medal on Beam at the 2008 Beijing Games. Shawn's infectious smile and electric performances made her an international media darling. Her athletic talents also helped her capture a "Dancing with the Stars" title after her success in Beijing.

Simon Porter

Born in 1993, Simon is a senior athlete competing for Canada. In 2011, he was the All-Around Champion at the Canada Winter Games in Halifax, Nova Scotia. In that same year, he was the All-Around silver medalist at the National Championships, and picked up 2 gold medals on Rings and Vault.

Simon:

"I began gymnastics when I was 3 years old. My parents signed me up because I was constantly climbing out of my crib and they couldn't control all the energy I had!

I did recreational gymnastics for 4 years before competing. I transitioned into the competitive world by going directly into the provincial stream. I was 7 years old at the time and did not know what to expect at all. My coach had told me countless stories of these 'mysterious' competitions, yet the idea of actually competing seemed like a fairy tale to me. This is why my first competition is still one my most exciting memories.

I have two important people in my gymnastics life who have been my role models and mentors. My coach, Norman Loader, has taught me for 13 years, since I was 5 years old. Gymnastics can be mentally challenging, and Norm has taught me how to cope with any challenges that may arise. For example, I love competing because I use it as an opportunity to show off the skills I'm working on, and the routines I've worked hard to perfect. I'm happy doing this, and winning or losing doesn't faze me at all.

Another role model of mine is Lukas Gataveckas. Lukas was one of the senior athletes at my gym, Toronto Gymnastics International, while I was growing up. He has since become a coach and a teacher, as well as a great friend. He's taught me a lot about having fun during training and competition, while staying on task and getting what needs to be done, done.

I also really admire Jordan Jovtchev because of his ring strength, and because of how long he has been competing."

Did You Know?... At 39 years old, Jordan Jovtchev has attended 5 Olympics and has qualified for a 6th.

Q&A

Simon's Goals and Dreams:
"To represent Canada at the 2016 Olympics."

Most Challenging Event:
"Parallel bars is my most challenging event because it requires the most technique. I am very strong and fast, which helps me to do big skills on floor, vault and rings. However, this means that I can use less technique on those events and do well. Generally, gymnasts who use power use less technique."

A Great Memory:
"The Canada Winter Games, in Yukon, 2007, was my favorite competition of all time. It was a two-week long multisport competition. There was a constant feel of energy everywhere I went. People from all over Canada came to watch and compete. Every province and territory holds CWG qualifiers to create multiple teams to send to the competition. Every placing during the games earns the province a specific number of points. Whichever province dominates with the most points, wins. In 2007, Ontario was only a few short points of first place. It came down to the final hockey game. Ontario won the CWG that year and everyone cheered and celebrated like there was no tomorrow! Also, I have met many people from that Competition who I'm friends with now and we often share and reminisce about the games."

A Funny Gymnastics Moment:
"When you train a lot, it's very easy to forget that you can do what you can because you've practiced it a thousand times. I learned this lesson the hard way. I thought I could do beam. This is a women's artistic gymnastics event, so I don't ever practice it. I got up onto the apparatus, called over my friends and said 'watch this!' On my first step, I lost my balance, fell flat on my back on the beam and rolled off the beam onto my face. It looked like a fall straight out of Saturday morning cartoons."

What Simon Loves About Gymnastics:
"I feel very strong and powerful on a daily basis. I also feel more energetic when I train regularly. If I miss a couple of weeks, I start to feel sluggish and lazy. This is one of the reasons I love the sport so much. When I think about gymnastics, I get an indescribable feeling. Asking me to narrow it down to one or a few things is impossible."

Bianca Dancose-Giambattisto

Born in 1994 in Chateauguay, Québec, Bianca Dancose-Giambattisto was a member of the 2010 World Championship team and Pan American Games team. She was 3rd at the 2011 National Championships, and has accepted a scholarship to the University of Florida.

Bianca:

"I was a very active and curious child, always climbing up the monkey bars at the park. At 4 years old, my mom signed me up for a toddler's gym course once a week. I started out in recreational gymnastics at age 5. At 8 years old, I started competing at the provincial level.

Cynthia Lemieux was my mentor. She trained with me until she moved to Chicago for college gymnastics last year. She has a tremendous competitive attitude that helped me and motivated me to work hard.

I want to represent Canada at the best of my ability in every international competition. My biggest dream has always been the Olympics. I am currently training to qualify for the 2012 London Olympic games.

I will always admire Nastia Liukin, the 2008 Olympic All-Around champion. She is an extremely beautiful gymnast with amazing lines. She tackles a high level of difficulty, especially on bars. I love the Russian gymnasts as well. They have a special spark and unique skills."

Q&A

Biggest Challenge:

"The most challenging thing for me is to be in the best shape, all the time. I have learned that I need to peak at the right time for different competitions. As I grow, I need to deal with the changes in my body."

Favorite Gymnastics Moments:

"My first World Cup in Qatar, where I won the bronze medal on bars, was an unforgettable experience. Another memorable competition was participating in the 2010 World Championships in Rotterdam. Being able to compete as a team, representing my country, is great. Interacting with gymnasts from all over the world, who share the same passion, creates a special feeling of connection."

Most Challenging Event:

"The most challenging events for me are vault and floor. They both demand a lot of power and speed."

Funny Gymnastics Memory:

"This is actually what got me into gymnastics in the first place: When I was only 2 years old, my mom had me wear a special padded helmet because I would jump and climb everywhere we went. Also, my mom first signed me up in ballet, but when I fell asleep in my first class, she quickly switched me to gymnastics."

Victoria Moors

Victoria:

"I got started in gymnastics when I was 3 years old. My parents put me in a class because I was always jumping on the furniture. When I was about 4 years old I was invited to try out for competitive gymnastics but my parents decided to keep me in recreational programs until I was 5. One day, Elvira Saadi, who is now my coach at Dynamo Gymnastics Sports Centre in Cambridge, saw me in the gym, and it wasn't long before I was training in a pre-competitive group. I trained for a few years, and began competing when I was 10 years old.

Elvira is my mentor. She has taught me everything I know about gymnastics and helped me learn how to push through hard days and have confidence in myself. She has believed in me during the times when I didn't.

I admire Russia's Viktoria Komova because she is an awesome gymnast."

Q&A

Goals and Dreams:

"I am hoping to qualify to represent Canada at the Olympics Games. When I am older, I want to become a coach."

The Most Challenging Thing About Gymnastics:

"Everything about gymnastics is challenging. On some days

Victoria Moors on the Floor Exercise at the 2012 Elite Canada, Mississauga, Ontario.

you have to give more than you can give, but you always have to try your best."

Favorite Gymnastics Moments:

"Competing in the London Olympics Pre-Test Event, winning a silver medal for the team competition event, and winning a silver medal in the Floor finals event. It was also very exciting to see the Canadian flag raised."

Funny Gymnastics Story:

"Just for fun, we like to make up men's floor routines in the gym."

Most Challenging Gymnastics Skill or Event:

"Right now, bars is the toughest event for me, because I have been trying to learn a new dismount."

What Victoria Loves Most About Gymnastics:

"Gymnastics has given me the chance to travel to different places around the world, like Russia, France and England. It's such a great sport because it always involves strength and beauty and inspires you to keep learning and challenging yourself. I can't imagine doing anything else."

Peng-Peng Lee

Peng-Peng:
"I was 4 years old when I was first introduced to gymnastics. I was a very energetic kid, always jumping on couches or climbing on furniture, so my parents put me into gymnastics. Both my parents did gymnastics when they were younger, so they naturally gravitated toward the sport. Also, my mom is a big believer in gymnastics as a basis for all sports.

At the end of my 8-week recreational program, my instructor referred me to the coach of the pre-competitive program. After I was tested for my gymnastics potential, I was accepted into the pre-competitive program at the age of 5. The pre-competitive program was very different than the recreational program because there was more focus on conditioning, strengthening and flexibility exercises instead of playing, jumping and swinging on the gymnastics equipment. The hours of training went up from 1 hour a week to 6 hours a week. I didn't enjoy the intensity and increased training hours, so I quit gymnastics when I was 7 years old.

After about a year and a half, my family moved from London, Ontario to Richmond Hill, Ontario. My mom looked into signing me up for new activities and asked if I wanted to try gymnastics again. I agreed, but only if it was for fun. We signed up with a local gymnastics club and that's when I fell in love with the sport. I rapidly learned a lot of gymnastics skills, and had so much fun doing them. I started competing in my first year at the new club, at the age of 9.

My coaches from Sport Seneca, Brian McVey and Carol-Angela Orchard, were instrumental in helping me become an elite, international-level gymnast. I started with them as a pre-novice gymnast and they not only taught me world-class skills, but also taught me how to conduct myself with class and pride, handle the different levels of pressures in competition, be respectful of the people involved, have good sportsmanship, how to deal with media and many other life skills.

The gymnast I admire most is Shawn Johnson. I love her style of gymnastics and how she can throw in all sorts of difficult skills. I also love how she always smiles on and off the competition floor; she seems like a genuinely happy person."

Canadian Peng-Peng Lee was a member of the 2011 World Championship team and Pan American Games team. She also participated at the 2012 London Test Event for the Olympics, where she placed 5th on Bars.

Q&A

Goals and Dreams:
"To go to the Olympics and win a medal for Canada. That has been the goal that has kept me motivated throughout my gymnastics career."

The Toughest Thing About Gymnastics:
"Injuries are definitely the most challenging thing about gymnastics. Injuries always interfere with life, and proceeding in gymnastics. When you're injured, you are usually dealing with pain, some type of debilitation, numerous medical and physio appointments, and rehabilitation. Also, when you are injured it is hard to accept that you will not be able to do gymnastics for a period of time, and that when you do return, you have to get back to the fitness and gymnastics level you were at before the injury. I have learned through my injuries, though, that it is critical to listen to your doctor and allow yourself time to heal, no matter how long, in order to return to gymnastics safely and fully."

Most Challenging Event:
"Beam is the most challenging event for me because it is hard to perform all the big tricks consistently in one routine. Also, competing on beam is so much different than training on beam, because in competition there are a lot of different factors that affect your performance, such as the brand of the beam, amount of nervousness to keep under control, the pressures you withstand to stay on the beam, and dealing with the distractions in the venue. I find beam to be the most mentally challenging event."

Best Gymnastics Moment:
"I loved it when Canada officially qualified a team to the 2012 Olympics at the Olympic Test Event in London, England. For the past year, I've had my sights set on qualifying a team to the Olympics because I really wanted Canada to be represented at the Olympics by a full team, and not by just one gymnast. All my training and focus have been on that one goal, so when it was achieved, it was monumental. I was extremely proud of how well my teammates competed that day. It was great being able to share that feeling of excitement, pride and celebration with all my teammates, coaches, fans and supporters. And, personally, I knew it was one step closer to my ultimate dream of competing in the Olympics."

A Funny Gymnastics Memory:
"Once, when I was doing a Yurchenko Double Twist and over-rotated to my back, my hair got stuck to the Velcro on the mat and I couldn't move. It took my coach 10 minutes to untangle my hair. It was hilarious."

What Peng-Peng Loves Most About Gymnastics:
"The experiences and opportunities that are associated with the sport are what I love most. I have had a chance to travel to places that I would have never visited, such as Rio De Janeiro, Tokyo, Doha, and Guatemala. I enjoy meeting new people from my travels and making new friends from all around the world. I love the experience of performing in front of different audiences and being in different venues."

CHAPTER 10

Competition: Raising the Bar

If you love the recreational gymnastics experience, you might want to take the sport to the next level: competitive gymnastics.

Lots of challenges—and very exciting times—lie ahead. Who are the greats who put gymnastics on the world stage? What can you learn from them? Who is part of the new generation of gymnasts leaping into a competitive career? What are the secrets to their success? And what does it take to get there?

I've also included all kinds of fun details about my own career, about what it was like to compete internationally, as well as things to watch out for and ways to cope with what can be a very demanding schedule. If you're interested in the world of competitive gymnastics, here are some things to consider.

Making the Transition from Recreation to Competition

The decision to progress to competitive gymnastics involves 3 parties: you, your parents and your coach. You may be ready to proceed if: you have mastered the skills taught in your recreational gymnastics class; you grasp new skills quickly, truly understanding the progressions in each move; and if you show consistency in your performance. Most importantly, though, you must be mentally ready: you have to love gymnastics! If you aren't, the long hours of training and the rigorous demands of competing simply won't be worth the sacrifice.

It's hard to believe how quickly competing took over my life. I went from training one hour a week, to 2 days a week for 3 hours a session, to 5 days a week for a total of 15 hours. And I was only 10 years old. Two years later, my hours doubled. By the time I was 14, I was away from home for 2 months of the year and even missed my prom. That lifestyle is not for everybody, but for me, it was a question of devotion. I was in love with gymnastics. Many athletes train at least 5 hours at a time, 6 days a week. That's 30 hours a week at the gym. On top of that, traveling to competitions around the world can consume another 2 months a year. This kind of commitment deeply affects other areas of your life, so think carefully about the consequences before you decide to become a competitive gymnast.

If this feels like the life for you, then read on!

Elfi Schlegel competing at an NCAA competition for the University of Florida.

I remember winning my first competition. I won a trophy for my efforts, while the second- and third-place athletes won medals. I was only 7 so my parents had to help me understand why I couldn't have a medal necklace like my friends!

How You Can Get Competitive

In the United States, after the recreational level of the sport, athletes can move into a level system, which consists of Levels 1 through 10. Level 3 is when you can start competing. After these levels, the next step would be to become a Junior, and then Senior, athlete.

In Canada, there is also a competitive level system that follows recreational gymnastics. If you have any questions about how these competitive streams are organized in your area, ask your coach or contact your regional Gymnastics Federation (see page 143 for contact information).

School

Gymnastics may feel like a world of its own, but getting a good education is also vital. You need to find a way to excel at both school and gymnastics. So, approach your teachers and your school administration and discuss your gymnastics schedule. They will have to provide you with homework to cover missed classes, grant extended homework deadlines and postpone tests. Also, in larger urban centers, there can be schools designed for elite athletes and their unusual schedules—these can be an interesting alternative.

Whenever I traveled, I would take my books and assignments with me. Then while I was away, I would take notes about my travels. When I returned, I would make class presentations about the countries I'd visited. I became a real pro at geography!

Simon Porter:
"When I was still in school, I managed juggling my workload and my gymnastics by using spares. During my spares, I would finish my work early and use a planner or an organizer to prioritize what schoolwork needed to be completed next."

Kyle Shewfelt:
"It took me 8 years to finish high school. I attended Calgary's National Sport School, taking one and a half years off to pursue my dream. The school was very flexible with my schedule and worked with me. I trained at Altadore Gymnastics in Calgary."

Family

I could never have embraced the world of competitive gymnastics without my family's support. As much as possible, try to be an active participant in your family's every day life. Do your share of the chores. Attend your siblings' extra-curricular activities.

My sister, Andrea, also grew to love and compete in gymnastics. She took up rhythmic gymnastics, where she excelled because of her flexibility and dance talents. We used to make up routines in our bedrooms and teach each other cool gymnastic tricks. I'll never forget when she came to do a demonstration at a University of Florida gymnastics meet, where I was studying on a gymnastics scholarship. She did an amazing rhythmic demonstration in front of 5,000 Gators fans. I remember thinking how lucky I was to share this passion with my sister.

Your parents will help transport you to events, and get you to the gym for those all-important workouts. A life in competitive gymnastics is a commitment for the whole family.

Financial Costs

When I decided to compete, my parents had to pay a lot of fees—club fees, gymnastic attire for competition, gas for driving to and from the gym. At the early stages of competition, there is no financial support for gymnasts. There may be a program set up with your club to fundraise or support young competitive gymnasts. It wasn't until I made the National Team that the Canadian government paid me a stipend every month to cover costs. Then, after I won a World Cup medal for Canada, the stipend doubled. It wasn't a lot—but it made me feel official, and eased some of the financial burden for my family.

Friends

Competing gave me the chance to make new friends, both at the gym and around the world. Meeting new people and learning about new places became my favorite part of traveling. And I still keep in touch with some of the people I met during that time.

But the truth is, having an exciting lifestyle can often be difficult on friends at home. They may feel left out—or left behind. Even if I sometimes felt far away from my school friends, I would try not to let distance get in the way. New telecommunication methods such as Skyping, texting, e-mail and instant messaging can keep you connected when you're traveling for gymnastics. Focus on what you and your friends share, not on what divides you. Don't forget to ask your friends about their lives. Celebrate their victories and be humble about yours.

Kyle Shewfelt:
"The life of a gymnast is challenging. You have to be so dedicated and work so hard. Sometimes it was tough to have friends who were living such different lives, going out to parties while I had to go to bed early to be ready for practice the next day. But gymnastics also made me feel empowered. And when I was training, all my friends were at the gym. They were my 'gym mates,' so it was easy to stay in touch!"

Bianca Dancose-Giambattisto:
"I'm different from other students because of the amount of school I miss for competitions and training camps. All my friends are very supportive and help me catch up with my schoolwork. I socialize with them mostly at school, because, with my busy schedule and all my competitions, I don't often get to see them out of school. But I still manage to communicate with them on Facebook and Skype. And of course I have many gym friends from all over the world with whom I love keeping in contact, also on Facebook and Skype."

Food

We discussed recreational gymnast nutrition in Chapter 4. Elite athletes have to focus even harder on feeding themselves properly, or they'll run out of energy during training or at meets. I remember, when I was competing, that breakfast was my favorite meal of the day. My mom always made me a bowl of oatmeal or cream of wheat before my competitions. On those days, I always felt nervous and didn't want to eat anything too rich. I felt satisfied eating this food... it wasn't fancy and gave me energy for a while. Of course, at meets, I always had some fruit on hand, like bananas and apples. Eggs were another food that didn't upset my stomach before a competition and provided good protein for long days in the gym or at a venue. Here is what other athletes eat during training or on competition days:

Emily Boycott:
"I pack protein bars, mixed nuts and seeds in my gym bag and I drink lots of water. I also eat some fruit. I like strawberries and kiwi. My mom doesn't like me to eat French fries, but I can have them for a treat when we go out."

Bianca Dancose-Giambattisto:
"I eat balanced meals. I need fruits and vegetables to give me energy. After every practice, I drink a protein shake to help me recover from training."

Peng-Peng Lee:
"There is no specific food that I eat to enhance my performance. But I generally eat a diet that contains proteins, whole grain carbohydrates, and vegetables, which gives me enough energy to last through my workouts. I always make sure that I consume protein within an hour after working out in order to repair my muscles. During competition I stay away from dairy because it may upset my stomach. There are many health benefits that come from gymnastics. I've experienced superior strength and fitness, great spatial awareness, good mental toughness, a greater ability to focus, and the discipline to eat healthier."

Victoria Moors:
"I eat lots of fruits and vegetables, as well as foods that are high in protein and fiber, but low in fat. Gymnastics has helped me stay in good shape and has taught me a lot about how to stay healthy and about how the body works. It has also given me a lot of confidence."

Shallon Olsen:
"I eat healthy foods such as cottage cheese, fruits and veggies. I like lots of yogurt and I've been called a 'giant mouse' more than once because I love cheese! Some of my other favorite foods are lychees, pomegranates and mangoes. Doing gymnastics keeps me fit and flexible. I know I can take part in physical activities and I won't be huffing and puffing. I like to do 'Just Dance' on my Wii and that keeps me in good shape too."

Simon Porter:
"Eggs and bananas really power me up and get me in the zone for competitions. I try to eat food with lots of proteins after training like meat and nuts. That helps a lot with my recovery."

Kyle Shewfelt:
"I was never very hungry on competition days, but apples were always part of my training. Then, after training, I ate a protein bar, eggs, or sometimes a sandwich."

Physical Therapy and Injuries
Increased training time often means sore muscles, and, sometimes, injuries. Physical therapy is a part of any competitive athlete's life. The goal is for you, your coach and a physical therapist to make every effort to keep you feeling good, strong and injury-free, as well as to prevent any injuries from becoming chronic.

To minimize the need for physical therapy, always warm up and cool down properly.

Coaches
The world of competitive gymnastics involves many people. Your personal coach may become a friend, a parent figure, even a role model. Competitive coaches want to maximize your talent and help you achieve new goals. This relationship may have ups and downs, especially considering how much time you will spend together. Be prepared for both good days and bad days. Sometimes you may not feel like training, but a good coach will have the ability to motivate you anyway. Communication between you, your parents and your coach is always the key.

Sports Psychologists

National team athletes sometimes work with sports psychologists. They can help you focus on your training through mental imagery—reviewing your routines the night before a competition, practicing breathing techniques and calming your nerves. Mental exercises can become a regular part of your routine, and almost as important as the physical training itself.

Judges

Competitive gymnasts receive an enormous amount of critical feedback from coaches, judges and other athletes. Dealing with a judged sport is not always easy. Regardless of your score, remember that you tried your best.

This image for the Shewfelt vault was taken from The Code of Points, the official gymnastics skills guide. Judges use these symbols to quickly notate different elements of a gymnast's routine.

25. Yurchenko tendu avec 5/2 t.
Yurchenko stretched with 5/2 t.
Yurchenko ext. con 5/2 g.
(Shewfelt)

6.6

The Code of Points book graphic of the Shewfelt Vault.

Competitive Training Schedule

At the senior Olympic level, many athletes will train 6 times a week, twice a day, anywhere from 35 to 40 hours a week. A lot of athletes keep a logbook to record their progress during training. I did. Every training schedule is different—athletes, their coaches and their families have to figure out what works for them. Here's a chance for you to compare several athletes' training regimens. What do you think would work for you?

Victoria Moors's schedule:

It's very challenging to balance training and competing with school, especially during the last few years, because I have to travel a lot for competitions. But I always try to do my best. Here's my competitive training schedule on an average day:

- ✔ 6:30 a.m.: Wake up, have high-fiber oatmeal with organic herbal tea
- ✔ 7:00 a.m.: Get dressed, check e-mail and pack for the day
- ✔ 8:00 a.m.: Tuesdays and Thursdays I have school until noon, then a light protein/fruit snack, then train at the gym 12:30 p.m.–5:30 p.m.
- ✔ Monday, Wednesday and Friday I have a full school day, then 3:30 p.m.–8:00 p.m. I train at the gym
- ✔ 4-hour regimen (alternately beginning 12:30 or 3:30 p.m.):
- ✔ Stretch for 15 minutes and identify current goals
- ✔ Conditioning for 30 minutes (stomach, arms, legs)
- ✔ Lines for 30 minutes
- ✔ Depending on the day, or whether I am close to competition time, I will work on different skills, like beam or bars; if I am close to a competition, I will do a shorter, more intense warm-up and do all four events for "mark"
- ✔ End of practice: half-hour conditioning, taking turns between leg and arm exercises
- ✔ Dinner: usually chicken, beef or salmon, with quinoa, vegetables and a rejuvenating fruit tea

- ✔ 8:00 p.m.: Arrive home, shower and try to rest before catching up on any homework or chatting with friends on Facebook or Skype
- ✔ 9:30 p.m.: Talk to coach on the phone about plans for the next day or about the months coming up
- ✔ 10:30 p.m.: Sleep

Shallon Olsen's weekly routine:
- ✔ Go to school in the morning and after lunch, hit the gym
- ✔ Train 5.5 hours per day on Mondays, Tuesdays, Thursdays, and Fridays
- ✔ Train for 3 hours every third Wednesday
- ✔ Train 5 hours on Sundays
- ✔ Most weeks I train 27 hours, which is grueling yet I enjoy it
- ✔ Do homework as soon as I get home from the gym each day
- ✔ Use Wednesdays and Saturdays to catch up on homework and school projects
- ✔ I work really hard to get good grades in school, and I also train really hard at the gym; it's difficult to juggle both because I miss 2 hours of school almost every day
- ✔ Downtime is important; I like to check Facebook, play computer games, watch gymnastics on YouTube, watch my favorite TV show, and use Wii
- ✔ When I am not in school, I am free to do as I wish; I like to visit with friends, hang out, go for walks with my mom or go to a movie

Kyle Shewfelt's typical training schedule before the Olympics:
- ✔ 6:30 a.m.: Wake up and eat breakfast
- ✔ 8:00 a.m.–10:00 a.m.: Training
- ✔ Snack
- ✔ 10:15 a.m.–12:00 p.m.: Training
- ✔ Lunch
- ✔ 1:00 p.m.–2:30 p.m.: Nap
- ✔ Snack
- ✔ 3:30 p.m.–6:30 p.m.: Training
- ✔ Dinner
- ✔ Catch up on e-mails; relax
- ✔ 10:00 p.m.: Lights out

Emily Boycott's typical training schedule:
- ✔ 9:30 a.m.: Wake up, have breakfast and get ready
- ✔ Hang out in my room, write stories or dance to music
- ✔ Lunch
- ✔ Travel 1 hour to the gym
- ✔ Train for 2.5 hours
- ✔ Drive back home and have dinner with my family
- ✔ At night I watch a movie and listen to music; I like to stay up late and get up late

Simon Porter's typical training schedule:
- ✔ Train 5 times a week
- ✔ Typical training day includes a warm up, skills and connections, as well as conditioning followed by static stretching for recovery
- ✔ Cross train outside the gym: including swimming, weight training and yoga
- ✔ Receive physiotherapy/chiropractic care twice weekly
- ✔ I also enjoy a busy part-time position at the gym coaching recreational, developmental and competitive boys

Peng-Peng Lee's typical schedule:
- ✔ I have finished high school and am taking a year off before university, so my training schedule is different this year
- ✔ I live far away from the gym so I train only once daily, Monday to Friday, generally 2:00 p.m.–7:00 p.m.
- ✔ Typical beginning: 1 hour of conditioning
- ✔ Each event: 45–60 minutes are devoted to each event
- ✔ End of practice: stretching and more conditioning
- ✔ Given my mornings are free during the week, I sometimes go to my local fitness club to do interval cardio exercises or back and core conditioning exercises
- ✔ Train Sunday 1:00 p.m.–5:00 p.m.

Bianca Dancose-Giambattisto's schedule:
- ✔ I'm in a sport-study program, so when I miss school for competitions my teachers are very understanding and help me catch up

- ✔ Attend school: 8:00 a.m.–12:00 p.m.
- ✔ Train: 1:00 p.m.–6:00 p.m
- ✔ Beginning: warm up and conditioning
- ✔ Each event: roughly 60 minutes are devoted to each event
- ✔ Finish up: basics and conditioning

Winning and Losing

Winning is great... but losing never feels that way. However, the healthy view on experiencing a loss is to consider it a great learning opportunity. Losing makes you a stronger athlete. It teaches you to dig down, identify what went wrong and learn how to improve your performance.

And winning isn't necessarily all it's cracked up to be. Being on top adds pressure. You're always looking over your shoulder at rivals and seeking ways to maintain your status.

Focusing on wins versus losses can lead to a black-and-white view of a sport.

Try to focus on progression, not perfection. If you didn't give your best performance, at least you gave your best possible performance at that moment. Give yourself a break. Enjoying the sport of gymnastics is not about how many trophies line your mantel. It's about improving the quality of your life with a sport that you love.

Trade Secrets, Superstitions and Good Luck Charms

In 1978, my mother and younger sister accompanied me to the Commonwealth Games in Edmonton. Before the All-Around finals, a ladybug landed on my leg. My mom was sure this was a good omen. Without letting on, she put the ladybug into a small jar along with some grass, poked holes in the lid and put it into her purse. That night, I won the Games. The reporters swarming around us asked my mother if she was proud. She showed them the ladybug in the jar and the reporters went crazy! They all wrote about my lucky ladybug. When we returned to Toronto it was to a mound of cards and presents, all with a ladybug theme. It's still my good luck charm.

Every athlete has 1 or 2 secrets they use to get through the pressures of competing. It might be a special food, a good luck charm, a special outfit or a ritual the morning of a meet. Here are some stories from a few athletes:

Peng-Peng Lee:
"I don't have any superstitions, but I do find that at some meets I'll decide to wear a certain pair of earrings, or a certain color eye shadow because it just feels lucky to me that day."

Elfi's scrapbook

Elfi Schlegel won team gold at the 1979 Pan Am Games.

I still cherish the success my team enjoyed at the 1979 Pan Am Games, but it's the friendship and bonds that I experienced with my fellow athletes that were the real reward.

Bianca Dancose-Giambattisto:
"I do not have any superstitions, but there are rituals... Before I leave for big international competitions, my grandmother takes me shopping, which relaxes me. At night before falling asleep, I visualize my routines perfectly executed. When I travel for competitions, I always bring 2 cards that both my mom and best friend gave me 2 years ago. They help me stay calm and composed when I get a bit too nervous. On my normal schedule, I watch motivational videos when I wake up in the morning, especially whenever I feel tired. When competitions are coming up, the videos motivate me to work extremely hard to reach my best fitness level. Nothing motivates me more than the thought of the Olympics. That is always in my mind."

Kyle Shewfelt:
"I didn't have any superstitions or good luck charms. But I did make a list of what I needed to remember the night before a competition. Then, on the day of the competition, I was always very quiet and very focused. I suppose my trade secret was that I always set goals for myself. It was part of my regimen. I set short-term goals and long-term goals, which gave me something to work towards and kept me on track. I think this is a big reason why I was successful."

Shallon Olsen:
"I don't have any superstitions about competing. I don't have any good luck charms either. But I have to do the splits before every competition. I also have to do 10 high kicks. I take 3 deep breaths to get oxygen into my blood and then I go and compete."

Victoria Moors:
"I don't have any superstitions about competing. As for trade secrets, I just try to be myself and stay positive and not give up on myself. I always try to do the best that I can on that day."

Simon Porter:
"At every competition I kick up to handstand and hold it for 10 seconds on the first try. One of my superstitions is around warming up too much. I try to keep all of my warm-ups short and sweet. If I feel like I'm having an off day or my head's not in the right place, I don't fight it. I will follow my basic training schedule and then leave the gym. It is so easy to get frustrated or demotivated when this happens. That is one of the reasons I have worked with my coaches and trainers to put together my basic training outline. It is simple to follow and I don't have to go all out in training. The most challenging thing is dealing with the emotions that come up during daily practice. Everybody knows how it feels to try something and fail. In gymnastics, the only way to learn a skill or learn how to connect elements into a routine is to try and fail, then try and fail again, until success. This can take 10 tries, or it may take 10,000 tries. Even after a new skill has been learned, it must be practiced repeatedly until it can be performed with near perfection. The way I deal with this is by treating my skill work as a scientist would treat his experiments. I try to keep my emotions clear and attack the skill with a new approach if I fail. I learned this technique from my coach, Norman Loader."

Shawn Johnson:
"I actually try not to have any. I'm always afraid if I have charms or rituals I will lose them or forget them, and then mess up! I do listen to music before I compete to calm me down, but that's about it."

Insider Tips

Each athlete has something that makes him or her tick. It may be a way of staying positive and upbeat, a way of staying motivated, or a way to get over a competition or routine that didn't go well. Here's a collection of great insider tips from these elite athletes:

Bianca Dancose-Giambattisto:
"My 3 tips are, work hard, always keep your big dream in mind, and have fun! The moment I jump on the bars, I feel a sensation of liberty. When I swing on the bars I feel untouchable, as if I could

fly away. The rush of adrenaline that fills me the moment the judge lifts the green flag, and sense of satisfaction at the end of an amazing routine, are incredible feelings unique to gymnastics that I will always love."

Simon Porter:
"1. Stick with it. Gymnastics becomes more fun as you get older. Sometimes, when you're young, kids think it's funny to poke fun at gymnasts. But when they get older, those bullies always wish they'd done gymnastics. 2. Never get frustrated. Compose yourself. If gymnastics were easy, it'd be called hockey. 3. Learn a standing back flip. Chicks dig flips."

Shallon Olsen:
"1. Concentrate on your gymnastics at all times. 2. Don't be nervous. 3. Have fun with it!"

Kyle Shewfelt:
"1. Start a journal. Write down everything you want to achieve: all the skills, and all the possibilities you see happening for yourself. 2. Don't freak out on a bad day. There are lessons in all mistakes. Making a mistake is when you have an opportunity to learn. 3. Don't be like everyone else—be different. Come up with something that separates you. Be innovative!"

Peng-Peng Lee:
"What has helped me in my gymnastics is that I always try to have a positive attitude in the gym. When I'm having problems with a skill, I make a conscious note of what I am doing wrong, but I don't dwell on that skill. I thrive on the process of thinking of new skills and then challenging myself to learn them. That's what motivates me the most. My 3 tips are: 1. Try not to compare yourself to your teammates, because everyone has their own special qualities and develops at their own rate. 2. Find a coach you like working with, and a gym you enjoy going to. 3. Always have fun, because if you are not having fun in the sport, you will never reach your full potential."

Victoria Moors:
"Keep focused on the goals you want to achieve each day, as well as the long-term goals you want to achieve. Always try your best, work hard and listen to your coach. But most of all, you have to love and have fun in gymnastics, because that's what will keep you coming back to the gym every day."

Emily Boycott:
"I have a little purple book that I look through before I compete. It has pictures of me with my medals and lots of positive thinking words like 'Believe,' 'I Can Do It,' 'I Love to Perform,' 'Smile, Smile, Smile' and 'Think Success.' I have these words hanging from the roof above my bed."

Shawn Johnson:
"Have as much fun as you possibly can and dream big! Gymnastics is such a powerful and beautiful sport. You have to put all your fears aside and find the confidence to defy gravity."

CHAPTER 11

Where Gymnastics Can Take You

Now you've read the inside scoop on the world of competitive gymnastics. Whether you choose this path or not, there are many other exciting options for staying involved in gymnastics. You can take your love, passion and knowledge of the sport and apply it in all kinds of great ways.

I trained very hard to become an Olympic-level gymnast, but I worked equally hard choosing my career path. I took my degree in television at the University of Florida and pursued a career in sportscasting. I also continued with my coaching, and went back to my roots in recreational gymnastics. Eventually, I opened my own gym with my sister. All the while, I took my knowledge for, experience in, and love of the sport and became a motivational speaker. So you can see that there are all kinds of ways you can stay involved in gymnastics—and make a living and a future for yourself. Consider the following careers:

Physical Education and Gymnastics Teacher

Using your passion for getting and staying fit is especially important in a school context—because you're sharing your message with young people. You can be a great role model for the next generation.

Television Sportscaster

Do you have a wealth of knowledge of the sport, who's involved, and who looks promising for the next World Championships or Olympics? Do you like being filmed? Do you converse clearly and with ease? Then this career could be for you.

Sports Journalist

Maybe you're not only a lover of gymnastics, but you're a great writer, too. If this is the case, becoming a sports journalist could be a great way to go. You may also get the chance to travel.

Researcher for TV, News or Radio

Maybe you want to work in sports journalism, but aren't suited for the limelight. Knowing statistics, keeping track of career trajectories and understanding everything about what's happening behind the scenes could be what makes you tick. In that case, being a researcher could be very rewarding.

Yvonne Tousek, retired Canadian National Team member, 1996 Olympic team member and Triple Gold Medalist at the 1999 Pan Am Games, performing here in Cirque du Soleil's show "Corteo."

Gymnastics Judge

If you know gymnastics scoring well enough to be able to evaluate other athletes' routines; if you're committed to fairness; and if you're quick-thinking during competitions, then this could be an exciting career. And you'll definitely travel with this job.

Sports Agent

Being a sports agent is an exciting combination of your knowledge of gymnastics and the world of business. Care for a roster of elite athletes, negotiate their contracts, and help shape their careers.

Motivational Speaker

If you are passionate about both gymnastics and communicating your ideas to others, then this could be a great job for you. Be a leader and motivate others to do their best for themselves and the sport.

Gymnastics Talent Scout

A talent scout is a person whose job it is to recognize and seek out talented athletes in the field of gymnastics, for a university team or a national team, or even an organization like Cirque du Soleil. It's a job that could mean adding travel to your regular workday.

Cirque du Soleil Performer

If you have gymnastics and acrobatic skills and you love to perform, being in the spotlight with an organization like Cirque du Soleil could be very exciting and challenging.

Dance Performer

Gymnasts are often also great dancers. If you love to put pieces to music and work with choreography, then you could appear on a competition dance show, and end up on primetime TV.

Stuntman or Stuntwoman

People who are good at leaps, bounds and twists can transfer their skills to stunt work, doubling for the stars in action sequences for film and TV.

Physical Therapist

If you would like to use medical skills to take care of athletes and help rehabilitate them from a physical injury, then becoming a physical therapist could be a great fit. Physical therapists, also known as PTs, are on site at major competitive events.

Athletic Trainer

An athletic trainer is a certified health care professional who works with athletes in the arena of injury and illness prevention, assessment and rehabilitation. You can work with an entire team or individual athletes.

Events Organizer

Do you have a love of gymnastics and also an ability to organize and coordinate people and events? Then becoming an events organizer could see you coordinating meets and gymnastics conferences.

Coordinator for the Olympics

The summer Olympics happen every 4 years—and need a massive amount of coordination. Olympics gymnastics events host athletes from hundreds of countries. Think of the logistics. You could be in charge of all those details... Imagine!

A Gymnastics Coach or Gym Owner

If you like the idea of managing a gymnast's growth, training and career, then being a coach might be a great way to go. Some people even dream of opening their own gym—I did, with my sister, Andrea.

Any of these exciting avenues can be open to you, with your love of gymnastics and an education. Put your heart into it, and explore where gymnastics can take you.

Elfi Schlegel and Andrea Goddard, owners of Schlegel's Gymnastics Centre, Oakville, Ontario, Canada.

Springing Forward

Success is not about winning an Olympic gold medal. It's about trying, learning and making an effort to push beyond a place where once you thought of giving up.

Each of us decides what our path will be. The sport of gymnastics has made me who I am today. It has given me a career, a community and a cause—to help others, but especially kids, to stay healthy, try new things, gain confidence and have fun. It has taught me many life lessons, such as determination, teamwork and perseverance. Those qualities are important in all aspects of life, not just sports.

I watch my own 3 children enjoy recreational gymnastics. I see all its benefits and how it has enhanced their lives physically, socially and emotionally. It has given them confidence to try anything, tackle anything!

I am looking forward to meeting the next child who embarks on that first recreational gymnastics lesson. That child will look at gymnastics with fresh eyes and an open heart. And with that point of view, anything is possible.

Glossary

Agility: ability to move quickly and with ease.

Apparatus: equipment used in the sport of artistic and rhythmic gymnastics. In artistic gymnastics the equipment includes the vault, bars, beam and floor. In rhythmic gymnastics the equipment includes rope, hoop, ball, clubs and ribbon.

Artistic Gymnastics: branch of gymnastics that involves performing various skills, such as vault, uneven bars, balance beam, floor, pommel horse, still rings, vault, parallel bars and horizontal bar on an apparatus.

Choreography: art of combining skill and dance elements to create a routine.

Code of Points: rules that govern the sport, made by the FIG and compiled in the Code of Points book. This book includes the skills used in artistic and rhythmic gymnastics. The Code of Points is updated every 4 years to allow for the evolution of the sport.

The "Def": one-and-a-half twisting salto skill on the high bar.

FIG: Fédération Internationale de Gymnastique. The organizing body for international gymnastics competitions, including the Olympics. FIG makes the rules, trains and certifies judges, and determines how competitions are run.

Giants: gymnastics skill performed by both men and women on the uneven bars, rings, parallel bars and high bar. From a handstand position, the gymnast makes a full 360-degree rotation, swinging downward and back up to a handstand position.

Glide kip: basic skill that is performed on the bars (by both men and women) and is used today as a connection skill in a routine. A glide swing progression is important to know prior to attempting this skill. (A glide swing plus a pull-up to front support is the basic kip action.)

The Horizontal Turn: a 360° turn on one leg, with the second leg in a forward horizontal position.

The Jaeger Salto: release performed by both men and women on the bars. The gymnast swings up, lets go of the bar, and performs a front flip to re-grasp the same bar. This is a full 360 rotation, and there are variations to this skill.

NCAA: National Collegiate Athletic Association.

NCCP: National Coaching Certification Program. A Canadian initiative designed as a standard for coaching development.

Preflight: position your body assumes when leaving the vaulting board, before touching the vault. In this position, you're airborne.

Re-grasp: action of letting go and catching the bars with your hands.

Rhythmic gymnastics: branch of gymnastics that involves performing various skills with apparatuses such as rope, hoop, ball, ribbon and clubs.

Routine: combination of movements displaying a full range of skills.

Salto: forward, backward or sideward rotation without the use of hands.

Standing Back Flip: from a standing position, jump in the air, rotating backwards in a tuck position landing back on your feet.

The Shewfelt Vault: vault derived from the Yurchenko vault (a round off onto the board, back handspring onto the vaulting table, with a double, twisting stretched flip), which adds an extra half-twist on the flipside. It was named after male gymnast Kyle Shewfelt.

Yurchenko Double Twist: round off back handspring onto the vault table, to a double twisting stretched flip.

Gymnastics Contacts and Web Sites

USA Gymnastics (USAG)

USA Gymnastics National Office
132 E. Washington St., Suite 700
Indianapolis, IN 46204
Phone: 317-237-5050 Fax: 317-237-5069
Website (USA Gymnastics Online):
www.usagym.org
USA Gymnastics Member Services
Phone: 1-800-345-4719
E-mail: membership@usagym.org

This is the official website of the United States Gymnastic Federation. It has information on the regions, states and clubs throughout the United States. It also offers biographies of current national team members in all gymnastic disciplines. It has information about the latest gymnastics events and news from around the world. It also features an event and television broadcast calendar. It provides links to other disciplines in the gymnastics family and to other gymnastics-related websites around the world, such as the Fédération Internationale Gymnastique (FIG).

Fédération Internationale de Gymnastique (FIG)

Fédération Internationale de Gymnastique
Av. de la Gare 12
1003 Lausanne
Switzerland
Phone: +41 21 321 5510
Website: www.fig-gymnastics.com
E-mail : info@fig-gymnastics.org

This is the official website of the Fédération Internationale de Gymnastique, also known as FIG. It is the world governing body for the sport of gymnastics. This website provides historical information, a guide to gymnastics, a glossary of terms, the rules that govern the sport, results of international events, a photo gallery, videos, newsletters, profiles and the world ranking of athletes. It also has links to the websites of gymnastics events around the world.

Gymnastics Canada Gymnastiques (GCG)

1900 Promenade City Park Drive, Suite 120
Ottawa, Ontario
Canada K1J 1A3
Phone: 613-748-5637
Website: www.gymcan.org
E-mail: info@gymcan.org

The Canadian Gymnastic Federation's website (offered in both French and English) includes information on all provincial federations, national team athlete profiles, competition results, a calendar of upcoming gymnastics events, news, press releases, and links to other gymnastics websites around the world.

Acknowledgments

Special thanks to all those involved in making this book happen: Debbie Boycott, Emily Boycott, Jean-Paul Caron from Gymnastics Canada, Grace Chiu, Tim Daggett, Bianca Dancose-Giambattisto, Jolie Dobson, Kirk Dunn, Marc Dunn, Andrea Goddard, Mary Howard from the University of Florida, Shawn Johnson, Ann-Marie Kerr, Leslie King and Luan Peszek at USAG, Peng-Peng Lee, Norm Loader, Victoria Moors, Dr. Larry Nassar, NBC Sports, Shallon Olsen, Triple Flip, Bernard Petiot and Katia Fiuza from Cirque du Soleil, Simon Porter, Philippe Silacci at the FIG, Rick Schell from SAsport, Kyle Shewfelt, Kim Uyeno from R.M.P. Athletic Locker, Rick Wilks, and the children who appear in this book: Catriona Currie, Cameron Dunn, Olivia Dunn, Evelyn Goddard, Annie Leonard, and Jessica Hardwick.

Index